CLARE CONNERY

QUICK & EASY

SALADS

BBC BOOKS

To 'Nannie' with love and thanks for everything

Published by BBC Books,
a division of BBC Enterprises Limited,
Woodlands, 80 Wood Lane, London W12 0TT

First published 1992
© Clare Connery 1992
Reprinted 1992

ISBN 0 563 36253 7

Designed by Peter Bridgewater
Photographs by James Murphy
Styling by Jane McLish
Home Economist Allyson Birch

Set in Bembo by Phoenix Photosetting, Chatham, Kent
Printed and bound in Great Britain by Clays Ltd, St Ives plc
Colour separations by Technik Ltd, Berkhamsted
Cover printed by Clays Ltd, St Ives plc

Front cover photograph: a mixed leaf salad of oak-leaf, lollo
rosso, curly leaf endive, radicchio, rocket, parsley, dill,
tarragon, chilli pepper and green and black olives. Back cover
photograph: Salad Kebabs with Spicy Dressing.

Acknowledgements

My sincere thanks to my commissioning editor, Heather Holden-
Brown, whose enthusiasm and encouragement made this publica-
tion possible, and to my editor, Anna Ottewill, for her support and
interest.

My gratitude is also extended to my friend and colleague of
many years, Ann Macfarlane, who has been both a joy and a
pleasure to work with and whose meticulous eye and attention to
detail ensured that the recipes were tested to perfection.

My thanks also to Doreen McBrien, my long-suffering secre-
tary, who continues to make sense of my handwritten scrawl, and
to Elizabeth Kirkpatrick, my catering companion, who ensured
that my clients were fed while I indulged in words and sentences.

CONTENTS

INTRODUCTION

Quick and Easy Salads tells you everything you ever wanted to know about salad ingredients, the equipment needed for a 'salad kitchen', and information on how to use and store these prodigious gifts of nature. I have concentrated on salads which include a wide range of salad leaves, vegetables, fruits, herbs and flowers from both the past and the present, ingredients all now readily available in the shops the length and breadth of the country, and in some cases even in our own back gardens. I have prepared these salads in both simple and sometimes exotic combinations to make nutritious and tasty snacks, first course dishes, main meals and desserts. There are salads for the busy housewife, mother, student and professional, which excite me and that I hope you will enjoy. My main purpose, throughout, has been to create salads that are tasty, interesting, sometimes unusual, but above all, salads that are 'quick and easy'.

About the author

Clare Connery is well-known to many through her successful BBC television series *Cook with Clare*, her mini-series – *Store-cupboard Cookery*, for BBC's *Bazaar*, and her regular appearances on *Daytime UK* and Yorkshire Television's *Farmhouse Kitchen*. She is also food correspondent for BBC Northern Ireland.

In 1986 Clare established a fine food shop in Belfast for which she won the United Kingdom's Delicatessen of the Year Award in 1987. In the same year, she opened a cookery school and expanded her successful catering company.

Clare Connery's previous books include *Irish Cookery with Magimix*, *Cook with Clare* and *Store-cupboard Cookery*. She is currently working on a comprehensive history of Irish food.

MY SALAD KITCHEN

Some of my most vivid and cherished memories are of my childhood summers spent at the home of my maternal grandmother in a small seaside town in County Down on the north east coast of Ireland. It was here in her cottage that I learnt to love the garden, its produce, and the art of self-sufficiency. In her tiny patch of land, my grandmother grew most of her food, supplementing her garden produce with only the smallest amount of extras. Fresh poultry and eggs were bought weekly from the local market and fish was delivered every Friday; exotic fruits and vegetables were somehow acquired from the enterprising greengrocer, all to be combined with the garden produce to create the freshest, most wholesome and delicious meals.

It was here that I learned the rudiments of self-sufficiency: how to prepare the soil, to dig and to plant, to harvest and to store all manner of vegetables, salad plants, herbs and fruit. It is only on reflection that I now realise how untypical my grandmother's garden was. Indeed many of the varieties I took so much for granted all those years ago, are only just beginning to appear in some of the larger shops.

Along with these kitchen garden memories remains the sight, taste and smell of its harvest. Every day there was something different. Sometimes it was a plateful of tiny vegetables, simply scrubbed and arranged in a kaleidoscope of colour on the plate; other times these delicate vegetables would be lightly steamed and dipped in freshly made butter. On occasions these simple meals would include chicken, fish or eggs, and when the weather turned wintery they would be combined into a robust stew. No matter what the meal, or where it was enjoyed, each had one thing in common: they were all accompanied by a big bowl of colourful salad leaves and herbs with a herb or fruit-flavoured dressing, or, in the winter, by a bowl of greens, cabbage or spinach. In addition we preserved the harvest surplus in bottles and jars, to enjoy for the rest of the year. It is only now that I realise the nutritional importance and value of eating these fresh, natural foods. These raw fruits, salad leaves and vegetables along with unprocessed seeds, grains and nuts are the richest natural source of vitamins, minerals and enzymes and unadulterated natural fibre; they also provide fine quality protein, easily assimilated natural carbohydrates and essential fatty acids, all nutrients vital for a healthy life.

Following my grandmother's tradition, in my own cottage, also in County Down, I tend my kitchen garden and do my cooking and writing amid pine and clutter. Although my 'salad kitchen', as it has become known, hasn't the purpose-built cupboards of my Belfast kitchen, it has everything I need. I make use of two refrigerators, one for general perishable foods, the other specifically for my vegetables and salad leaves. Such chilled storage is invaluable, particularly if you aim to produce healthy meals with speed and, like myself, are unable to shop every day. It is of course not necessary to have two refrigerators: one good sized unit is adequate. In addition, I also have storage space for my 'dry goods' such as seasonings, flavourings, nuts, seeds, dried herbs, grains and pasta, and also my flavoured vinegars and oils.

The equipment needed to produce quick and easy salads is minimal: a few pots for boiling rice, pasta and grains, along with a large frying pan and wok for stir-fries and risottos, and a steamer for cooking vegetables when required. My one mainstay is the food processor. This speeds up so many kitchen processes and saves such a lot of time and energy that it is ideal for the quick and easy salad kitchen. I use the metal cutting blade for practically everything: chopping vegetables, grinding nuts and seeds and homogenising vegetables for soups, as well as for making dressings, dips and pastry. The grater is perfect for vegetables, cheese and fruit, for muesli and salads, and the slicer is ideal for vegetable preparation for many different salads. A liquidiser or blender is also useful, but it does not have the versatility of the food processor. A coffee grinder is useful for grinding small quantities of nuts, herbs and seeds.

Other essential tools include several sharp knives in different sizes; a good sharp vegetable peeler and vegetable scrubbing brush; a large and small chopping board; a salad spinner; several mixing bowls of varying sizes; a small selection of wooden spoons, spatulas, a ladle, slotted spoon, heavy wire whisk, measuring jugs and kitchen scales. For storing prepared food, heavy duty polythene bags or rigid containers with lids are also useful.

Many of the dishes in this book were created in my 'salad kitchen', dishes I have been preparing for years both for my family, friends and catering company; many I made originally in my grandmother's kitchen with her to guide me. They are all recipes of which I never tire, and I hope you, too, will not only enjoy them but use them frequently in your own kitchen. As we say in Ireland, *Slaite mhaith* – your very good health!

NOTES ON THE RECIPES

Follow either metric or imperial measures for the recipes, not a mixture of both. All spoon measures given are for either metric or imperial measuring spoons which give accurate measurements for small quantities.

All recipes serve four people except where otherwise stated.

Three different sizes of onions have been used in recipes. Their approximate weights are as follows:

LARGE, 200–225 g (7–8 oz);   MEDIUM, 150 g (5 oz);   SMALL, 75 g (3 oz).

Sizes of cartons, packets or tins have been given as printed on the products used in testing the recipes. Use the nearest size available to you.

In the recipes, I have suggested the use of olive or sunflower oil, however other oils can be used depending on personal preference.

Where possible the recipes use fresh herbs. When these are not available use half the quantity of dried herbs.

Where cartons, packets or tins are used the exact measurements found on their labels are given. Always use the nearest size available.

BASIC SALAD STORE-CUPBOARD

As demand for a wider variety of produce increases, shops have been encouraged to stock an increasingly varied range of products. More and more people now have the opportunity to sample a wide variety of salad ingredients and some grow their own requirements in kitchen gardens. Salads are no longer entirely regarded as 'rabbit food'. Emphasis is now placed on simplicity and flavour coupled with the desire not only to be visually appealing, but nutritionally sound. Today's salads strive to be fresh, unadulterated combinations of bright lively colours and varying textures and tastes. There are other ingredients which combine well with salad leaves to produce complete dishes: vegetables in their raw and cooked state, herbs, spices and flowers, sprouted seeds, nuts, grains and cereals, pulses and pastas, dairy produce, meat, poultry and game, and of course oils and vinegars for the all important dressings. To use these ingredients to the full and combine them successfully, it helps to know and understand them, particularly those which form the basis of a quick and easy salad store-cupboard.

SALAD LEAVES

Salad leaves can be divided into three main groups, the traditional 'lettuce' leaves, 'other leaves', and the family of brassicas (or cabbage).

LETTUCE LEAVES

Lettuce can be divided into three categories; the cabbage, the long-leaved and the loose-headed varieties.

Cabbage-type lettuce These include the *round heart* or *butterhead lettuce* which has loose fine textured leaves on the outside, generally with a lightly packed heart in the centre, similar to the cabbage itself but with much more delicate leaves and with a slight sweetness to the taste. Two varieties for the kitchen garden are 'Tom Thumb', a quick-maturing miniature head with slightly crumpled leaves, and 'Trocadero', which has green leaves tinged with red.

The *crisp head* or *cabbage head lettuce* is also included in this group. These varieties have large, very tightly packed heads of pale green leaves which were originally bred for uniformity, crispness and shelf life. Although they have rather a bland taste, the advantage is that they stay crisp, will keep well for several days, and are excellent when used as the base of a salad along with some of the more unusual leaves. The best known variety is the 'Iceberg'.

Long-Leaved Lettuces These have elongated heads of rich green oval leaves and a crisp pale green heart. They are known as Cos or 'Romaine'. Like the iceberg lettuce they also have the ability to remain crisp but they have a much more pungent flavour and more interesting texture than the cabbage heads.

Loose-headed or loose-leaved lettuces These are perhaps the largest group within the lettuce family, embracing all the lettuces which do not have particularly obvious heads. They vary in colour and depth of flavour from the delicate, sweet, mild taste of the frilly-edged *red leaf* and *green leaf lettuce*, to the deep, rich flavour of the highly prized *oak-leaf lettuce* with its gently ruffled leaves of deep olive-green brown, tinged with dusty pink. In addition there is a variety of loose-headed lettuce called 'Salad Bowl', which produces a great profusion of leaves but no heart, and which is practically non-bolting.

OTHER LEAVES

The group of leaves referred to as 'other leaves', includes members of the chicory and endive family, various salad greens and cresses, along with edible wild leaves such as purslane and dandelion. They are highly valued for their flavour and the variety of colour, shape and texture that they bring to all leaf salads throughout the year. The largest single group of these belongs to the chicory family.

Chicory There are dozens of varieties of chicory, with just as many uses – ranging from salads themselves to a coffee substitute! To confuse things even more, chicory is often referred to as endive. The Belgians call it *witloof* (white leaf), the French and the Americans call it endive, and the British, chicory. Whatever the name, or the variety, they are generally available throughout the year, but are most valued for use in winter salads when the more delicate salad leaves are not so readily available.

Belgian chicory is a native to Europe and western Asia, but is also grown in America where it is known as *Belgian endive*. It grows from the root of the plant which is first cultivated outdoors, then forced and blanched inside in peat and total darkness. It produces a compact conical head of crisp, white/yellow leaves about 13–25 cms long known as 'chicons'. It has a pleasantly bitter flavour and a crunchy texture which combines well with other milder more delicate leaves, but is also distinct enough to be eaten on its own. The faintly bitter flavour may be lessened by removing and discarding the plant's core.

Chicory, also known as *curly leaf endive* and *chicoree frisée*, is native to southern Asia and northern China. It has a low-growing head of large curly, frilly-edged leaves which range in colour from a rich deep green on the outside to a tightly packed centre of pale lemon/green tendrils, when the plant has been left in the dark for several weeks. This 'blanching' not only bleaches the colour of the plant but mellows the slightly bitter taste of the dark outer green leaves.

Escarole is another member of the chicory family and is also known as *broad-leaf endive* and *Batavian endive*. It has flat frilly leaves which are firm in texture and slightly bitter in flavour. It is a hardy plant and is excellent for winter harvesting either as an entire plant or a few leaves at a time. This cut-and-come-again technique will often produce a second and third crop.

Radicchio also known as *red Verona chicory* and *tallarosa*, is from Italy. It has a small compact head of ruby red leaves tinged with white, and although slightly bitter in flavour, is becoming increasingly popular, particularly because of its bright colour. Very little is needed to enhance a salad bowl or plate and it keeps well if stored in the refrigerator.

Rocket This is more correctly known as *arugula* but is also referred to as *roquette* and *rugula* and is noted for its fiery, spicy, slightly peppery flavour and characteristic tartness which combines well with milder greens. It should be eaten young, when its smooth notched green leaves are small and delicate, and certainly before the plant flowers, when its leaves will turn tough and bitter. In Mediterranean countries it grows wild and is an essential ingredient of *mesclun*, the provincial mixture of small salad greens.

Lamb's lettuce This is also known as *mache* and *corn salad*. It has small, round deep green velvety leaves with a mild and refreshing flavour. It should be harvested when small and tender, before flowering, as a complete plant or as outer leaves only. This promotes new growth from the centre of the plant.

Winter purslane Also known as *claytonia* and *miner's lettuce*, this is an excellent winter salad plant and has a pretty leaf shape and a fresh mild flavour.

Purslane This is a garden weed rarely found in shops, but it can of course be cultivated from seed. The leaves are small and spoon shaped, and grow in a rosette shape from a fat juicy stem which spreads rapidly across the soil.

Salad burnet This is a low-growing hardy perennial plant which grows in clumps in poor sandy soil. The pretty lacy leaves which remain green all winter are rounded with slightly serrated edges. When young and tender they have a refreshing cucumber taste which combines well with other salad leaves.

Dandelion Although despised by many a gardener, the dandelion's long, deeply notched leaves, with their tart astringent butteriness, are highly prized by salad cooks particularly in France and Italy where they are grown commercially. They can be blanched like chicory, or their leaves, roots and flowers can be chopped into salads. When grown from seed, they generally produce larger leaves with a more mellow taste. Dandelion leaves are at their best in spring when the leaves are young and pale green and before the plant comes into full flower. After June they tend to become coarse and bitter.

Sorrel Another edible wild plant, sorrel looks very much like a small dock with its pointed spear-shaped leaves. It is one of the first green plants to appear in spring, universally found in moist damp areas. It is sometimes called *dock* and *sourgrass* because of its sharp astringent flavour. This sharp lemony taste makes them an interesting addition to a salad.

Spinach Like sorrel, spinach has a pleasant acidic – but less strong – taste due to oxalic acid. It also has bright green leaves which when young are deliciously tender and highly nutritious. Spinach has the advantage over many salad vegetables in that it can be grown throughout the year.

Spinach beet Also known as *perpetual spinach*, this produces a succession of fresh leaves over a long period, only turning to seed during its second year. It is the easiest to grow of all spinach crops.

New Zealand spinach This is a summer vegetable which grows in branches and enjoys poor, dry soils. It has thick, fleshy leaves with a trailing habit.

Swiss chard Also known as *silver beet* or *seakale beet*, Swiss chard, like spinach, is easy to grow and is often regarded as a spinach substitute although it has an entirely different flavour.

Cresses A member of the nasturtium family, watercress has smooth round leaves, slightly hairy crunchy stems and a strong peppery taste. It grows profusely along streams and springs in limestone-rich areas, but care must be exercised when picking it to ensure that it is watercress and not its lookalike companion, marshwort or foolscress, which is poisonous. It is important that the stream or river is free flowing, fresh and unpolluted. Watercress can also be easily grown in the garden as long as it gets plenty of water. It perishes very quickly and lasts longest with its stems in water and its head in a polythene bag. *Landcress* Is an annual plant, also known as *American* or *winter cress*, which will provide peppery flavoured leaves all year round. It enjoys a dark damp spot in the garden and after sowing will provide aromatic bright green clusters of serrated leaves in about eight weeks. The outer leaves should be picked first, leaving the centre to produce more; as the plant gets older, leave the outer leaves and pick only those from the centre. Landcress makes an excellent substitute for cress, but has a slightly less delicate flavour.

BRASSICAS

The third and final group of salad leaves belongs to the family of brassicas or cabbage, the best known of these being the firm compact-headed cabbage with smooth leaves of green, white or red. They are most widely available in winter and are particularly useful in salads where the more delicate salad leaves are not available. *Chinese cabbage* is a most valuable salad plant as its strong yet delicate yellow-green overlapping leaves have a crunchy texture and a long shelf life.

SALAD HERBS

Even the most attractive and delicious of salad leaves are enlivened and enhanced by the use of culinary herbs and flowers. Their aromatic leaves, with crunchy or delicate textures, and their infinite variety of colour and flavour can transform an everyday salad into a sensuous experience. Herbs such as fennel and dill add piquancy to salads, while robustly flavoured leaves like lovage add body and an earthy quality; basil, coriander, dill, mint and balm help aid digestion.

Packets, bunches, even pots of many types of fresh herbs are now widely available in many shops; plants or seeds can be bought from garden centres and nurseries. Growing herbs for the kitchen requires only limited space in a sunny position either outdoors or on a windowsill.

BASIL

This wonderful, clove-flavoured and fragrant herb combines beautifully with salad leaves, and is an essential ingredient in Italian pesto (p. 43). It has a great affinity with tomatoes and produces highly flavoured butters, oils and vinegars. It does not dry well and is therefore very much a fresh summer herb, best grown in pots. There are two main types, *common or sweet basil* with its medium to large-sized strongly flavoured leaves, and the *Greek, bush basil* with its smaller, finer leaves and slightly milder flavour. As well as these two main types there are also *lemon-scented* and *purple-leaved varieties*.

BORAGE

This beautifully decorative herb with dull green hairy leaves and bright cobalt blue star-shaped flowers grows wild in many parts of Europe and England and is known as the 'herb of courage'. Both the flowers and the very young leaves have a sweet refreshing flavour like cucumber and are used to enhance a green salad and to make a tisane or herb tea.

CHERVIL

Chervil, like fennel, is a sweet aromatic herb with a mildly aniseed flavour. Its delicate fern-like foliage can be used liberally in salads and when chopped it is often used as a slightly grand substitute for parsley. Chervil is one of the herbs used with parsley, chives and tarragon in the mixture known as *fines herbes*. It makes excellent herb vinegar and remains green in winter which makes it invaluable in the salad kitchen.

CHIVES

Like parsley, chives are one of the most widely grown and frequently used herbs, both for taste and decoration. The delicate onion flavour is used to enhance sauces, egg dishes and salads. The pretty mauve flowers, appearing in July and August, make an attractive garnish.

CORIANDER

The delicate, flat, parsley-like leaves have a very distinctive taste and earthy pungency that makes them most memorable and delicious in salads. The small round seeds with their warmly aromatic flavour are more widely used finely-ground as a seasoning.

DILL

The delicately flavoured leaves of dill, with their unique spicy green taste, are delicious sprinkled among salad leaves. When chopped and added to mayonnaise or oil and vinegar, they make an excellent dressing. The flower head of this annual herb is used to flavour pickled gherkins and herb vinegars.

FENNEL

This aniseed-flavoured herb, with its feathery fronds and chopped stems, imparts an interesting texture and flavour to salad dishes, marinades and mayonnaise. Its bright acid-yellow lacy head also makes an excellent salad garnish.

GARLIC

The strong, unique flavour of garlic is indispensable in the salad kitchen. A cut clove rubbed round a salad bowl imparts a subtle flavour to salad leaves. Peeled cloves are used in marinades for vegetables, fish and meats. Crushed cloves are an important part of many salad dressings and make a fine-flavoured vinegar or oil. Garlic is widely available, and when fresh and firm it will store well for many months or even years.

LEMON BALM

The small round leaves of lemon balm with their attractive and refreshing lemony flavour are excellent in salads, either as whole leaves or finely chopped. It also makes a calming tisane or herb tea.

LOVAGE

Like fennel, lovage is a tall attractive herb which is most decorative both in the flower and herb garden. Its dark green, indented, glossy leaves and stalk closely resemble celery, as does its flavour which is very strong and distinctive. Both the leaves and stalks should be added sparingly to salads.

MARJORAM AND OREGANO

There are many forms and varieties of this tender sweet-scented thyme-like herb. There is *sweet* or *knotted marjoram*, which is annual and has soft leaves; *pot marjoram*, which is perennial and has less fragrant leaves, and *wild marjoram*, which is also known as *oregano*. Oregano has a more pungent flavour than marjoram, with slightly darker green small leaves which look very pretty.

MINT

The distinctive taste and smell of mint is perhaps one of the most well known of all the herbs. There are many varieties, including apple mint, spearmint, peppermint, raripila mint and pineapple mint. Depending on the flavour required, they can be used sparingly in leafy salads and other salad dishes to impart their special 'minty' flavour.

PARSLEY

This is one of the most important culinary herbs and its mildly flavoured leaves, in both the common *curly type parsley* and the more aromatic flat leaf or *Italian parsley*, are widely used both for flavouring and decoration. The stalks have a more concentrated flavour than the heads and are an important element in a classic *bouquet garni*, along with a bay leaf and a sprig of thyme. Parsley is also an important element in the mixture of finely-chopped herbs referred to as *fines herbes*, along with chervil, tarragon and chives.

SAVORY

There are two main forms of savory, the annual *summer savory* with its white flowers, and the perennial *winter savory* with its pale lavender flowers. They both have small, spicy leaves with a flavour similar to thyme. Winter savory has a slightly milder flavour and is a more compact plant. Both can be added to salads, but use sparingly.

SWEET CICELY

The delicate, lacy, fern-like leaves of this tall, pretty herb have a sweet taste reminiscent of aniseed and liquorice. The young leaves, either chopped or left whole, make an excellent addition to a salad. Sweet cicely, like angelica, has a sweetening effect on acid fruit. Its root can be boiled and used sliced in salads.

TARRAGON

This perennial summer herb, with its long narrow leaves, is highly prized for its aromatic, mildly aniseed flavour. There are two forms of this herb – the smaller leaved and more distinctly flavoured *French tarragon* and the taller, coarser and larger leaved *Russian tarragon*. I prefer to use the French tarragon, particularly for including in salads; chopping with parsley, chervil and chives for *fines herbes*, and for making salad dressings and herb flavoured vinegar.

SALAD FLOWERS

Food should be appealing not only to the taste buds, but to the eye, and although some flowers such as nasturtiums and pot marigolds are used for their flavour, they are mainly used to provide a wonderful contrast both in colour and texture to any food. With salad leaves, however, they are quite stunning, and make an excellent conversation piece at any table.

When using edible flowers in salads, make sure they are clean and free from poisonous insecticides. They should be gathered early in the day when they are at their freshest and the dew has just dried off their blooms. If picking wild flowers from the fields and meadows, pull only those that are plentiful and take care not to uproot the entire plant. Those protected by law, such as English cowslips, should not be picked and the more common varieties, like cow parsley, should be gathered in moderation to conserve nature's beauty.

Not all flowers used in salads are wild; many are cultivated flowers such as carnations, primroses, violets, roses, honeysuckle and, of course, nasturtiums and marigolds. Whether cultivated or not, it is important to know which are edible and which are poisonous, particularly since some of the most beautiful and appealing are deadly. I have listed a few of those which I find most useful and attractive and which are, of course, edible. For further information on others, it is best to consult a specialist book on edible flowers.

Before use, flowers should be shaken well to remove any insects, and gently rinsed under fresh running water to wash away dust. They are very fragile and need to be handled carefully, and lightly patted dry with a paper towel. They should then be kept in a closed plastic bag in the refrigerator until required. Dip in iced water before adding to a previously dressed salad.

BORAGE

The brilliant cobalt blue star-shaped flowers of this annual herb look marvellous and taste sweet. Before using, remove the hairy sepals behind the petals.

CHIVES

The attractive mauve flowers of chives, which appear from June to August, make colourful additions to salads – either in whole heads or individual petals.

CHRYSANTHEMUM

In China and Japan, special varieties of young chrysanthemum flowers are fried in batter and served in soups, but the many forms of the florist's chrysanthemum can also be used. Before use, the flowers should be dipped in boiling water for a few minutes; the petals are then sprinkled on the salad.

COWSLIP

The yellow flowers of this perennial plant are used whole in salads.

DAISY

The pretty little white lawn and field daisies can be used whole in salads. They look much prettier open than closed, so need to be picked in sunshine just before use. The petals of the larger cultivated varieties are sprinkled over salads, their pink, red and white petals adding a splash of colour to the leaves.

ELDER

This hedgerow shrub produces the most delightful lacy sweet-smelling blossoms, composed of tiny confetti-like flowers, in early summer. A few shaken over a salad just before serving will give a delicate musty flavour.

GERANIUM

The blooms and leaves of the many varieties of pelargoniums (geranium) plant, including rose, lemon and peppermint, have a mild delicate flavour; leaves added to salads are attractive and tasty.

LAVENDER

This Mediterranean shrub with its tiny purplish-blue flowers along tall, spiky stems, is very strongly flavoured and both the flowers and chopped leaves should be used sparingly in salads.

LOBELIA

These attractive flowers, with their bell-shaped blossoms, have a faintly sweet smell, reminiscent of honeysuckle. They are available in a variety of colours – ranging from white or pink to shades of blue, and look most colourful sprinkled through a salad.

POT MARIGOLD

These should not be confused with African or French marigolds. In salads, only the pot marigold petals should be used. They come in all shades of orange and yellow with double or single flowers. They have long been used in cooking and salad preparation for their fairly strong flavour and bright colour.

NASTURTIUM

The blossoms of these brightly coloured annuals are beautiful, ranging from red to bright yellow and orange. They are available in trailing and dwarf forms and the leaves which are plain and variegated are equally attractive and delicious to eat. The leaves have a peppery taste and the flowers and flower buds a peppery piquancy. The seeds are picked as *capers*.

PANSY

These pretty perennials, with their velvety textures, bright faces and marvellous range of colours, can flower all the year round, to bring interest and attraction to any salad. The small varieties can be used whole.

PRIMROSE

Primroses are perennial plants; their bright yellow flowers, similar to cowslips, can be used whole in salads.

ROSE

Any rose, whether wild or cultivated, can be used in salads, but the more aromatic the rose, the more sweet and delicate will be the flavour. The petals add colour and fragrance when sprinkled over a salad.

SAGE

The purplish-blue, pink and white flowers of this narrow-leafed herb add colour and fragrance to salads.

VIOLET

The whole flowers, stems and leaves of the violet are edible and look very pretty in salads. They combine well with lettuce and onion. Their delicate blossoms in purple and pink have a slightly sweet, spicy flavour.

Many other flowers are edible and can be used in salads. Here are the names of some of the most common and familiar: camomile; red clover; cornflower; courgette; dandelion; honeysuckle; lime blossom; lovage; rosemary and thyme.

SALAD VEGETABLES

In addition to this wide variety of salad leaves, herbs and flowers, there is a natural storehouse of many exciting vegetables which can bring additional life, texture and colour to the salad. Like the salad leaves, these are often more enjoyable eaten raw than when cooked. Their taste is fresher, their colour and texture preserved, and without doubt their nutritional value is also retained. Such vegetables will generally have a longer store-cupboard life than their rather more delicate leafy relatives.

Vegetables regarded as being traditionally 'salad vegetables' and quite naturally served raw, such as tomatoes, cucumber, celery, peppers, radishes and beetroot, can also be joined by other raw vegetables: fennel, celeriac, kohlrabi, carrots, parsnips, turnips and brussels sprouts, sliced, shredded or grated; peas and broad beans podded only; mushrooms and mange-tout peas, left as they are or sliced; green beans along with courgettes and leeks, sliced or diced; and cauliflower, broccoli and calabrese, broken into florets.

These raw vegetables – whether with floppy leaves, compact heads or minature florets; whether diced, grated or sliced – if fresh and in peak condition, eaten quickly or stored carefully, are the richest and cheapest source of the many vitamins and mineral elements essential to our health and well being.

FRESH FRUITS

Fresh fruits also have an important nutritional role to play in the creation of 'quick and easy' salads. Like fresh vegetables, fruits are an important source of certain vitamins, particularly vitamin C, and also have a varied selection of minerals and lots of dietary fibre. Fruit also adds colour and variety to all sorts of salads, both savoury and sweet. There are a number of recipes for these throughout the book and a special chapter on 'fruity' salads. As far as my salad storecupboard goes, there are some fruits like apples, oranges, lemons, grapefruit, pears and dates that are always in stock; others like grapes, mangoes, pawpaws, melons, pineapples, kiwi fruit and the wonderful berry fruits of summer, only make an appearance when they are in season, for a specific dish or a special occasion. The choice you include in your store-cupboard collection, as with the vegetables and salad leaves, is very much a matter of personal taste and preference, but variety is important.

SALAD STORE-CUPBOARD
ADDITIONS

In addition to these fresh natural salad ingredients, there are other foods which, when combined with salad leaves, fruits and vegetables, can turn a light dish into a delicious substantial and filling feast for the whole family. Here are some that I find most useful in the quick and easy salad store-cupboard.

PULSES

These are also known as *legumes* and are the dried seeds of podded vegetables such as peas, beans and lentils. They are an excellent store-cupboard vegetable with a shelf life of six to nine months and can now be readily found. They are available in both dried and canned forms; the latter is generally more expensive but is by far the quickest way to use them. I have used a mixture of both in the recipes because only the red kidney and haricot beans are available in small size cans. Dried beans, with the exception of mung and black-eyed beans, need to be soaked overnight, then drained and boiled fiercely for the first 10 minutes to kill the toxins . Lentils and split peas do not require soaking. Some of the most useful bean varieties are listed overleaf.

Butter/lima bean A large creamy white or pale green bean, is usually available in two sizes, one slightly larger than the other. They have a soft floury texture and a mild flavour which combines well with salad leaves and herbs. They require 60 minutes cooking time.

Haricot bean The most widely known but probably the least interesting in this extensive family. It requires 60 minutes cooking.

Cannellini beans Small, creamy white, kidney-shaped beans which cook in 75 minutes. *Flageolet beans* are small pale green beans and cook in 45 minutes. *Red kidney beans* are sweet-tasting beans and come in many colours ranging from dark pink to maroon. They require 75 minutes cooking time. *Barlotti beans* are speckled, vary from cream to pink, and take 60 minutes to cook; the smaller *pinto beans* are also speckled pink and brown, and take 75 minutes to cook.

Mung beans Small olive green beans which, when cooked for 45 minutes, can be used whole in salads. They are more generally known and used in their sprouted form as 'bean sprouts' (see p. 108).

Chick peas Large dried peas, usually golden in colour. They are very attractive in salads, and used to make the popular Middle Eastern salad dip, Hummus. They take about 2 hours to cook.

CEREALS, RICE AND PASTA

Bulgar or cracked wheat This is the main cereal I use for salads, particularly Tabbouleh, a Lebanese salad (see p. 46). When soaked it can be used raw.

Rice A particularly useful store-cupboard ingredient for salads, rice can be combined with many of the salad vegetables and leaves to make substantial and tasty dishes. I keep three types of rice in my store-cupboard: long grain, white and brown rice. A combination of white and wild rice is now fairly readily available. Long grain white patna rice will cook in a large pan of boiling water in exactly 11 minutes. Wholegrain (brown) rice requires 20–40 minutes depending on the brand. For the white and wild rice combination it is best to follow the packet instructions as the times can vary.

Pasta This is one of the most versatile foodstuffs in the store-cupboard and some of the most attractive and colourful salads I make use many of the hundreds of different varieties of pasta now widely available both fresh and dried. The many shapes can be made either from refined or unrefined wheat, plain or naturally coloured with spinach or tomato. Fresh pasta can be stored either in the refrigerator for a few days or in the freezer for 4–6 weeks. Dried pasta has a much longer shelf life and will keep for several months. Dried pasta takes 6–12 minutes to cook depending on the type. Tagliatelle and fettuccine usually take about 6–8 minutes; the bows and other shapes, and macaroni, take up to 10 minutes, and spaghetti 12 minutes. Wholewheat pasta needs longer. Fresh pasta needs much less time, only 2–3 minutes.

NUTS

Nuts are a useful addition to salads because they add taste and texture and are very nutritional. Keep at least a small selection (peanuts, hazelnuts, pine nuts or walnuts) in the salad store-cupboard in airtight jars where they will keep for several months. Nuts can be used either raw or roasted in salads.

SEEDS AND SPROUTS

These are also useful additions to salads, adding taste and texture. The most useful seeds for salads are sesame, pumpkin and sunflower, used plain or roasted. The most commonly used seeds and grains for sprouting are alfalfa, adzuki, barley, fenugreek, lentil, mung, pea, soya and wheat (see p. 108 for details on how to sprout these).

FLAVOURINGS

Flavourings, whether they be fresh herbs or flowers, or indeed the wide range of powders, liquids and pastes readily available from the shops, are the ingredients which help to produce an infinite variety of salads, dressings and sauces, and are an essential part of any salad store-cupboard.

Peppers and salt *Black pepper* is an invaluable asset in any kitchen, but particularly that of the salad kitchen where it adds flavour and aroma to entire dishes and almost every salad dressing. Pepper should be freshly ground just before use otherwise it loses its pungency. *Paprika pepper* is a sweet, slightly hot spice, adding colour and flavour to many salad dishes particularly those using rice, as well as salad dressings. *Chilli pepper* is the hot powdered fruit pod of the capsicum plant and needs to be used with care. Added to salads and dressings, it makes them hot and fiery.

Salt is one of the basic seasonings in salads and salad dressings, but use it in moderation. Sea salt is naturally iodised and has no added preservatives. It is available coarse or fine. Grinders can be used for the coarse kind.

Mustards *English mustard powder* when mixed to a smooth paste with a little water or vinegar makes an excellent addition to salad dressings and mayonnaise. *Dijon mustard* is a French mustard with a totally different flavour to English mustard and indeed other French mustards. It makes an excellent addition to salad dressings. *Meaux mustard* is also a French mustard, but made from whole crushed mustard seeds which gives it a very grainy texture and a deep spicy flavour. It is also a valuable addition to salad dressings.

Sauces, oils and vinegars Soy sauce is made from soya beans, flour and water, which is then fermented and aged for some months. There are two main types, light and dark. The dark soy sauce has been aged much longer, which accounts for its much darker colour and stronger taste. I generally use the light soy sauce, preferring either the naturally fermented *shoyu,* or the Japanese version called *tamari,* which contains no chemicals and has a much better flavour.

Tabasco is made from chillies, vinegar and salt. It is a thin fiery sauce with a long shelf life. Only a few drops are required. *Worcestershire sauce* is a rich spicy sauce made from an old Indian recipe which includes soy sauce, vinegar, molasses, chillies, tropical fruit and spices. A useful addition to salad dressings.

Oil is one of the most important ingredients in the salad kitchen, for it forms the basis of the many rich and varied dressings and mayonnaises which help to complement salad dishes. There are many different types including olive, sunflower and corn oil. These and others are fully discussed in Chapter 5 (p. 91).

Vinegar is an essential ingredient in salad dressings and comes in many different flavours and strengths. These are also discussed in Chapter 5 (pp. 93–95).

In addition to these 'essential' salad ingredients, there are a variety of other items which are equally important, and not only enhance salads but which will extend their range. Items like canned fish, some canned meats and vegetables and a range of exotic canned fruits like mango and lychees are useful. Dill pickles, olives and capers add sharpness to many salad combinations. Spices and other aromatic seasonings often turn the ordinary into the exotic and Mexican taco shells or pitta bread make excellent containers for the impromptu salad creation. In my refrigerated store, I keep natural yoghurt, tofu (white bean curd made from soya beans), cottage cheese, blue cheese, cheddar cheese and cream cheese, eggs and bacon. In the deep freeze I will usually have a few chicken breasts, a piece of roast beef and some prawns for a 'meaty' type salad.

SALAD STORAGE

Most leaves, vegetables, fruit and herbs required for salads should be bought and used as fresh as possible, as they only lend themselves to being stored in the refrigerator for a very short time. Salad leaves, before storage, need a little special care to extend their life and maintain their quality and nutritional value. Any dead or wilted outside leaves should be removed. If the lettuce is clean, put it directly into a loose-fitting polythene bag; if, however, it is dirty or the leaves are going to be used later in the day, separate them from the stalk and wash them gently under cold running water before drying in a good salad spinner or basket, before placing in the bag. Sealed airproof wrappings and containers will prevent the leaves from breathing and cause them to rot. Store in the salad drawer of the refrigerator. Very delicate leaves like lollo rosso, oak-leaf lettuce and curly endive, can be stored root down in a bowl of water in the refrigerator with the head loosely covered with a polythene bag. This keeps them fresh and crisp for several days. An excellent remedy for wilting leaves is to submerge and soak them in a large bowl of cold water for 2 hours before use. The leaves will return to their original crispness. Leaves can remain in water for up to two days without showing any signs of deterioration. More robust leaves like 'Iceberg', Chinese leaves and the cabbage varieties will keep for about seven days in the refrigerator. Fresh herbs can be stored in the same way.

Carrots and parsnips will also keep well in polythene bags in the bottom of the refrigerator or in a cool larder. They are best packed, unwashed, which seems to keep them fresh longer.

Most fruits can be stored in the refrigerator where they will of course remain fresh, but less ripe, for longer. Berry fruits need to be refrigerated as soon as being picked or purchased, as they deteriorate very rapidly.

I only use deep freeze storage for animal products that can be used to produce more substantial and varied salads.

SALAD STARTERS

When salads are used at the start of a meal, they should excite the palate and stimulate the appetite for the courses that are to follow. As a result, they must be light and attractive to look at, carefully arranged on the plate to create a composition of colour and texture, but they should not be so substantial that they appease hunger.

First course salads can be made with any type of salad leaves or a variety of vegetables such as sticks of raw carrot, cucumber, courgettes, celery and other crisp vegetables, served with a dip or dressing and known as *crudités*. Salad leaves and varying shapes of all types of vegetables can also be combined together to make a crisp crunchy colourful collation.

First course salads can also be more complex affairs, with the leaves acting as a base for small portions of other ingredients such as meat, fish, poultry or cheese. Ideally these should be prepared in fine slices, thin slivers or small cubes, and added lightly to the salad, cold or warm. In the latter case, along with a hot dressing, the result is known as *salade tiède*. When salad leaves are used for the base of a first course salad it is generally sufficient to allow about 20 g (¾ oz) per person. Adding a little more and using a larger plate, you can easily turn these salads into quite substantial main course dishes.

No collection of first course salads would be complete without including tomatoes, particularly in a book with my name on it. Tomato salads, of all varieties, as long as the tomatoes are firm and well flavoured, are one of my greatest pleasures. Use tomatoes simply sliced, or if cherry size, cut in half, sprinkle with fine quality virgin oil, a quick grind of black pepper and more than a sprinkling of fresh basil leaves.

When the highly scented and well flavoured charentais and ogen melons are in season they make admirable companions for the tomato as does the more humble cucumber (see p. 27). Sliced tomatoes can be layered with finely sliced onion and red pepper rings, moistened with a little vinaigrette dressing and of course a sprinkling of herbs such as fresh basil, parsley and oregano. This salad in particular is not only excellent as a first course with crusty bread, but as a salad to accompany main course dishes, and is a valuable element in a selection of salads on a cold buffet table.

The slightly sharp, acidic flavour of tomatoes also combines well with the creamy smoothness of avocado pear. When both are sliced, and arranged slightly overlapping each other on a bed of young leaves, they provide a refreshing introduction to any meal.

TOMATO SALAD WITH FETA CHEESE AND BASIL

S E R V E S

—— 4 ——

INGREDIENTS

2 Mediterranean or beef
tomatoes or 16 cherry
tomatoes or 6 average
size, well flavoured
tomatoes
200 g (7 oz) feta cheese
Freshly ground black
pepper
3–4 tablespoons olive oil
Small bunch of fresh basil
leaves

As a first course or a light lunch, this dish has few rivals.

If using Mediterranean or beef tomatoes, remove the stem, and cut in slices about 3 mm (⅛ inch) thick. Arrange the slices on a large serving dish or individual plates.

Cut the feta cheese into 1 cm (½ inch) cubes and scatter on top of the tomatoes. Season lightly with the black pepper and sprinkle with a little oil.

Tear, rather than cut or chop, the basil leaves into fine strips and scatter over the top of the salad. If time permits, leave loosely covered in the refrigerator for about 30 minutes to enable the flavours to develop before serving with crusty bread.

TOMATO, MELON & CUCUMBER SALAD

S E R V E S

— 4 —

This light and refreshing, yet simple salad, made with whatever well-flavoured melons and tomatoes are in season, makes an excellent first course particularly on a warm summer's evening. When the honeydew melons are at their tastiest, they offer good value for money. However, the ogen, charentais and cantaloupe melons, with their sweet fragrant flesh, although smaller and more expensive, are generally much more reliable. Galia melons, when ripe, are also sweet and flavoursome. It can be simply served in soup cups, or on flat plates covered with a loose arrangement of green leaves such as lamb's lettuce and watercress. Garlic and herb bread is served as an accompaniment and is a useful means of mopping up the fruit and vegetable juices.

INGREDIENTS

1 small melon, or half a honeydew
450 g (1 lb) tomatoes
½ cucumber
1 tablespoon parsley, finely chopped
1 tablespoon basil, finely chopped
1 teaspoon snipped chives
6 tablespoons French dressing (p. 95)
Freshly ground black pepper

Cut the melon in half, remove the seeds and either scoop out the flesh with a large vegetable ball cutter or remove from the skin and cut into cubes.

Quarter the tomatoes or cut into pieces the size of the melon. Combine the fruits and vegetables in a mixing bowl.

Mix the herbs together and add half to the salad in the bowl, reserving the remainder to sprinkle on the salad before serving.

Pour on the French dressing and add a little black pepper. Toss the salad lightly but thoroughly in the dressing, cover and chill for several hours to develop the flavours. Serve with the juices in soup cups or in the centre of a selection of loosely arranged leaves on a flat plate, sprinkled with fresh herbs.

Tomatoes Stuffed with Guacamole

SERVES
— 4 —

INGREDIENTS

4 medium tomatoes
1 ripe avocado
2 tablespoons lemon juice
2 drops of tabasco sauce
A pinch of chilli powder
½ tablespoon onion, peeled and finely chopped
Salt and freshly ground black pepper
Mixed salad leaves
A few small basil leaves to garnish

Guacamole, a spicy Mexican purée made from avocado pear, lemon juice and chilli powder, makes an excellent dip or a light stuffing for well flavoured tomatoes. Served on a base of mixed salad leaves and accompanied with fingers of hot toast, it makes an attractive and tasty first course. As avocado pear discolours quickly, it is best not to make the filling too far ahead. The speed at which it will discolour will depend on its degree of ripeness. When choosing an avocado, make sure the skin is free from dark coloured patches and bruises and that it feels slightly soft when gently squeezed at the stalk end. Avocados are very delicate so be careful when testing for ripeness or it could mean a bruised avocado for someone else.

Cut a slice from the rounded end of the tomato, about a quarter of the way down. Reserve this for decoration. Scoop out the seeds and some of the flesh from the remaining tomato with a teaspoon, taking care not to damage the delicate tomato shell. Discard the seeds and chop the flesh. Place into a bowl.

Halve the avocado, remove the stone and scoop out the flesh. Place in another bowl with the lemon juice, tabasco sauce, chilli powder, onion, salt and pepper. Mash with a fork until the consistency is creamy and smooth. Add the tomato flesh and adjust seasoning to taste. Divide the mixture between the four tomato shells.

Arrange the washed and dried salad leaves on medium plates and set the stuffed tomato on one side. Garnish with the tomato top and fresh basil leaves. Serve chilled.

PEARS IN
TARRAGON DRESSING

S E R V E S
— 4 —

There are many varieties of pear throughout the world, differing in size, colour and texture and used for eating fresh, cooking and preserving. The best known home-grown dessert varieties, all of which are suitable for this dish, are Williams, available in late summer, and Commice or Conference in early autumn. All these have a juicy white flesh that is both slightly acid and sweet to the taste, with a strong but pleasant scent. In this recipe, peeled half pears are set on a bed of small, delicate and colourful leaves such as baby butterhead lettuce hearts, lamb's lettuce, watercress, arugula, oak-leaf lettuce, red chicory, or young dandelion leaves, before being coated with a tangy tarragon-flavoured dressing. A variety of two or three leaves is sufficient.

Begin by preparing the dressing. Put the egg in a bowl and beat to break it up. Gradually whisk in the vinegar and sugar. Set the bowl over a small pan of simmering water on a gentle heat. Beat continuously with a small balloon whisk. At first the mixture will look very frothy, but gradually as the egg cooks the bubbles become smaller and closer until they have amalgamated into a thick smooth mayonnaise-type sauce. Remove from the water and leave until cold. Stir in the yoghurt, tarragon and enough pepper to flavour without overpowering.

Just before serving, arrange a selection of salad leaves on four medium size plates. Peel the pears and cut in half lengthwise, removing the core, pips and fibrous threads. Set a pear half on each plate, in the centre of the salad leaves, and spoon enough of the tarragon dressing over each pear to just cover. Sprinkle with a few fresh tarragon leaves and add some borage flowers to the lettuce if available. The deep purple blue colour helps the salad to sparkle. Serve chilled with wholemeal bread or cheese biscuits.

INGREDIENTS

FOR THE SALAD
2 large ripe dessert pears
75 g (3 oz) mixed salad
   leaves
1 teaspoon fresh tarragon
   leaves
A few borage flowers
   (optional)

FOR THE TARRAGON DRESSING
1 egg, size 3
2 tablespoons tarragon
   vinegar
¼ teaspoon caster sugar
65 ml (2½ fl oz) thick
   natural yoghurt
2–3 tablespoons fresh
   tarragon, finely chopped
Freshly ground black
   pepper

SALAD KEBABS WITH SPICY DRESSING

SERVES

— 4 —

FOR THE SALAD

8 mange-tout peas, topped and tailed

7.5 cm (3 inch) piece of cucumber, cut into 2 cm (¾ inch) chunks

8 large mushrooms cut in half or 16 button mushrooms

8 cherry tomatoes

½ red pepper, cut approximately in 2 cm (¾ inch) pieces

4–8 black or green stoned olives

75–100 g (3–4 oz) mixed salad leaves (endive, oak-leaf lettuce, watercress)

FOR THE DRESSING

8 tablespoons sesame oil

4 teaspoons balsamic vinegar

1 teaspoon tamari sauce

½ teaspoon tabasco sauce

½ teaspoon lemon juice

1 clove garlic, peeled and crushed

(8 × 14–15 cm (5½–6 in) kebab skewers)

A variety of fresh crunchy vegetables and fruits can be combined on a wooden kebab stick about 14–15 cms (5½–6 inches) long for a mixed hors d'oeuvre. Vegetables such as mushrooms, cherry tomatoes, cucumber and courgette chunks, mange-tout peas, celery, fennel and red, yellow and green pepper pieces all skewer well, as do orange segments, apple, pear, melon and banana pieces and individual fruits such as strawberries, raspberries, dates and apricots. Diced tofu, pitted olives, and cheese can also be added. The savoury and sweet fruits and vegetables can be kept quite separate for either savoury or dessert dishes, or combined for the more flexible first course. Serve with a spicy dressing.

Prepare the kebab vegetables by wiping, washing and cutting into suitable size pieces where necessary. Wash and dry the salad leaves and divide between four medium plates. Thread the vegetables on the skewers, giving an attractive balance of colour, flavour and texture. Lay two skewers on each plate on top of the mixed leaves.

Prepare the dressing by combining all the ingredients in a screw-top jar and shaking well to form an emulsion. Serve with the kebabs, spooning a little over each skewer and the mixed leaves.

CRUDITES

Crudités is the general name given to a collection of crunchy raw vegetables and salad leaves eaten with the fingers and served with a light dressing, sauce or dip. Firm washed and dried vegetables and leaves such as carrots, celery, cucumber, peppers, fennel, chicory, spring onions and lettuce hearts can be cut into finger length pieces or sticks; tight-headed vegetables such as broccoli or cauliflower can be broken into florets; small whole vegetables like cherry tomatoes, mushrooms, mange-tout peas, green beans and radishes can be left just as they are. The prepared vegetables are then arranged in groups on either a large serving plate or individual plates.

A selection of two or three dips, sauces or dressings such as a light French dressing, a garlic mayonnaise or a chick-pea dip are offered separately. A wide selection of these are given on pp. 91–107. The number and variety of the vegetables and dressings is totally dependent on individual tastes and requirements. However, I generally allow a total of 100–150 g (4–5 oz) of mixed vegetables per person.

Crudités can also be served as a light lunch with wholegrain bread, when obviously a large quantity and variety of vegetables would be served.

WARM CHICKEN LIVER SALAD WITH RASPBERRY DRESSING

SERVES
— 4 —

INGREDIENTS

FOR THE SALAD

100 g (4 oz) mixed salad leaves (e.g. lamb's lettuce, batavia, lollo rossa and rocket)
50 g (2 oz) fresh raspberries (optional)
1 tablespoon olive oil
6 chicken livers

FOR THE RASPBERRY DRESSING

1 clove garlic, peeled and crushed
1 tablespoon pink peppercorns, crushed
2 tablespoons dry sherry
4 tablespoons raspberry vinegar
4 tablespoons olive oil
A pinch of salt

Warm salads (*salades tièdes*) have become increasingly popular in this country over the last few years as stylish starters, although they have been served in France for many years. They combine a selection of interesting and colourful leaves with a more substantial ingredient such as chicken or duck livers, scallops, bacon or prawns. The leaves are loosely arranged on a medium plate and the main ingredient lightly fried in a little olive oil before being arranged among the leaves just prior to serving. The dressing, consisting of usually a little more oil, flavoured vinegar or sherry, is then added to the hot pan, quickly blended with the pan juices and immediately poured over the crispy leaves. The success of such salads depends on light cooking and quick service.

Wash and dry the salad leaves and divide between four medium plates with the raspberries, when in season. Heat the olive oil in a frying pan and fry the washed, trimmed and dried livers until brown on the outside but slightly pink in the centre. Remove from the pan with a draining spoon and keep warm.

Add the garlic and peppercorns to the pan and fry for a few seconds before pouring in the sherry. Stir to blend with the liver juices. Add the vinegar, bring to the boil and reduce the liquid by half. Gradually whisk in the olive oil and season with salt.

Cut the chicken livers into bite size pieces and arrange among the salad leaves dividing them between the plates. Scatter the fresh raspberries on top. Pour the warm raspberry dressing over and serve immediately.

SALAD KEBABS WITH SPICY DRESSING (PAGE 30)

MANGE-TOUT SALAD WITH CHICKEN LIVERS AND BACON

SERVES

— 4 —

This fresh colourful spring salad combines the delicate flavour of warm chicken livers and bacon with crisp fresh vegetables and lightly scented herbs. I use mange-tout peas along with a selection of salad leaves for their crisp but tender texture and their sweet delicate taste. These sugar-peas, or snow peas as they are sometimes called, have no waste, only needing to be topped and tailed. If very short, they can be left whole, otherwise cut them in half diagonally. Radishes and radicchio add a peppery bitterness which also makes an excellent contrast to the sweetness of the peas. The leaves and vegetables are combined and tossed in a simple French dressing before being topped with the meaty ingredients.

———

Combine the prepared vegetables and salad leaves in a large bowl and toss lightly to mix. Prepare the dressing by combining all the ingredients in a screw-top jar and shaking well to form an emulsion.

Wash and trim the livers, dry well and cut in half. Fry the liver and bacon in the hot oil until the bacon is crisp and the livers just cooked. While they are frying, toss the salad in the dressing and divide between four medium plates. Remove the liver and bacon from the pan using a draining spoon and scatter over the dressed leaves. Sprinkle with fresh coriander leaves and serve immediately.

INGREDIENTS

FOR THE SALAD
100 g (4 oz) mange-tout peas, topped and tailed
4 small radishes, sliced in circles
A few leaves of radicchio, torn into pieces
A small crisp lettuce heart, torn into pieces
1 bunch of watercress
A handful of pale yellow curly endive fronds
4 chicken livers
4 back bacon rashers, rinded and chopped into 1 cm (½ inch) pieces
2 tablespoons olive oil
Fresh coriander leaves to garnish

FOR THE DRESSING
65 ml (2½ fl oz) olive oil
2 tablespoons red wine vinegar
1 clove garlic, peeled and crushed
Salt and freshly ground black pepper

GREEN BEAN SALAD (PAGE 48) AND CURRIED PASTA SALAD (PAGE 42)

SPINACH AND DANDELION SALAD WITH BACON AND CROUTONS

SERVES

—— 4 ——

INGREDIENTS

FOR THE SALAD

50 g (2 oz) small young spinach leaves

50 g (2 oz) young dandelion leaves

100 g (4 oz) lean bacon, cut into 1 cm (½ inch) slices

FOR THE DRESSING

1 clove garlic, peeled and crushed

¼ teaspoon Dijon mustard

½ tablespoon wine vinegar

1 tablespoon olive oil

Salt and freshly ground black pepper

FOR THE CROUTONS

1 slice of white bread, with crusts removed and cut into 5 mm (¼ inch) cubes

2 tablespoons olive oil

Young dandelion and spinach leaves are crisp and delicate with slightly bitter but refreshing flavours. Although dandelions grow wild throughout the countryside and in many city gardens, those grown from commercial seeds have fleshier leaves and a less bitter flavour. If the plant is covered with an upturned flower pot for a few weeks before cutting (blanching), they will taste even less bitter. Curly endive leaves are very similar and make a good substitute for the dandelion leaves. The spinach leaves should be small and very young. This salad can also be made entirely from either spinach or dandelion leaves.

Remove the spine from the spinach leaves if necessary and wash with the dandelion leaves in cold running water. Dry in a salad basket or spinner. Tear the leaves in half, if large, and refrigerate in a polythene bag until required.

To make the dressing, put the crushed garlic in a wooden salad bowl, add the mustard and half the wine vinegar, stirring to blend. Gradually work in the olive oil until quite thick. Season to taste with the salt and pepper.

To make the croûtons, fry the cubes of bread in 1 tablespoon of hot olive oil until an even golden brown. Remove from the pan and drain on absorbent paper.

Cut the bacon slices into 5 mm–1 cm (¼–½ in) cubes or slivers and fry in the remaining hot oil until crisp.

Put the salad leaves in the salad bowl with the dressing and toss lightly. Add the croûtons and bacon cubes. Put the remaining ¼ tablespoon wine vinegar into the pan with the bacon juices, swirl the pan to combine and pour over the salad. Divide between four medium plates and serve immediately.

SALADS ON THE SIDE

With many wonderful varieties of salad leaves now so readily available throughout the year, there is no need for any salad to be dull. Indeed, the choice of salad leaves, vegetables and complementary ingredients is such that a fresh, tasty arrangement can be quickly produced and used anywhere on the menu.

One of the principal ways of serving salads on the side is as accompaniments to main course dishes, as plain leafy arrangements. These are generally composed of a single type of salad leaf or a number of different varieties skilfully combined and simply dressed. These salads can also be served on their own at some stage during the meal, as is done in France, to refresh the palate between courses. There are no hard and fast rules as to what should go into these leafy salads, just fresh crisp leaves, well balanced in colour, taste and texture.

Other types of vegetables provide a stimulating range of materials with which the creative salad cook can work. These can be used raw to make popular salads like Coleslaw (p. 49) and Curried vegetable salad (p. 59), or more complex constructions like the Chinese salad on p. 58. When cooked, these vegetables produce an entirely different result, still referred to as salad, and equally delicious. They range from single vegetable dishes such as the popular Potato salad (p. 60), to the perhaps less familiar dish of mixed vegetables in a spicy cooked dressing known as Vegetables à la grecque (p. 66).

Pasta, rice and beans also play an important part in the creation of many salads to be served on the side with cold main course dishes like meat roasts, vegetables and nuts, or fish. All these salads form an important element in the formation of a cold buffet table, and when carefully selected and well balanced in colour, texture and taste, make a wonderfully decorative contribution.

A CLASSIC GREEN SALAD

S E R V E S
—— 4 ——

FOR THE SALAD
1 bunch of watercress
1 crisp round lettuce,
  prepared as on p. 22
Some fresh chives and
  parsley, chopped

FOR THE DRESSING
6 tablespoons olive oil
2 tablespoons wine vinegar
2 cloves garlic, peeled and
  crushed
1 teaspoon salt
Freshly ground black
  pepper

The success of any salad depends on the quality and freshness of the ingredients along with their careful preparation and garnishing. The green salad, whether simple or elaborate, is no exception. Any variety of leaves can be used, alone or in combination (with herbs or flowers, depending on the season and availability), together with a light oil and vinegar dressing complementary to both the leaves and the main course. Once the leaves have been selected they require careful separating, washing and drying (see p. 22). For this classic green salad I have used one of the most readily available lettuce, the round or butterhead lettuce, with a very simple French dressing. More varied dressings are given on pp. 95–99.

Discard any discoloured watercress leaves. Tear any large lettuce leaves into big pieces, leaving the crispy heart in individual leaves. Place together with the watercress in a large salad bowl.

Prepare the dressing by combining the ingredients in a small screw-top jar and shaking vigorously to form an emulsion; adjust seasoning for taste and sprinkle over the leaves. Toss lightly to coat the leaves and sprinkle with the chopped herbs. Serve immediately.

NASTURTIUM & CHRYSANTHEMUM LEAF SALAD

S E R V E S

— 4 —

This is one of the most delicious salads both to eat and to look at. Nasturtium leaves have a refreshing sharp-hot flavour and chrysanthemum leaves offer a slightly acidic and pungent taste when combined. Tossed in a walnut dressing and garnished with brightly coloured nasturtium flowers, they make a stunning summer salad.

Carefully wash and dry the salad leaves and make sure that the flower heads are free from dust, soil and insects, washing if necessary. Tear the nasturtium and chrysanthemum leaves into large pieces and separate the lamb's leaves from their stalks. Toss together in a large salad bowl.

Sprinkle the dressing over the leaves just before serving and toss to coat well. Then add the nasturtium flowers and serve immediately.

INGREDIENTS

6 large nasturtium leaves
8 chrysanthemum leaves
50–75 g (2–3 oz) lamb's leaves
2 tablespoons Walnut dressing (p. 96)
4–8 brightly coloured nasturtium flowers

MESCLUN SALAD

S E R V E S

—— 4 ——

200 g (7 oz) small mixed salad leaves
1 small clove garlic, peeled and crushed
⅛ teaspoon Dijon mustard
4 tablespoons olive or hazelnut oil
1 tablespoon white wine vinegar
Salt and freshly ground black pepper

'Mesclun' is the provincial name for a mixture of small delicate salad leaves such as rocket, lamb's lettuce, oak-leaf lettuce, curly endive, romaine, red radicchio, dandelion and some herbs such as chervil and flat-leafed parsley, although there is no individual formula. Some of these leaves are now available from good shops. To be sure of a supply, however, they are best home grown in a window-box, or a garden. I grow several varieties of these salad leaves from the salad mixture 'Saladisi', sometimes described in seed catalogues as a cut-and-come-again crop. This enables me to cut a few leaves at a time, thus allowing the plants to continue to grow and hopefully bring forth one or two further crops.

Wash and dry the salad leaves carefully (see p. 22). Put the garlic and mustard into a large salad bowl, preferably wooden, and mix to combine. Gradually add the oil and the vinegar, continuing to mix until well blended. Season to taste with salt and freshly ground black pepper. Add the salad leaves and toss lightly until well coated with the dressing. Serve immediately.

*W*INTER LEAF SALAD

S E R V E S

—— 4 ——

In the winter when the wide variety of leaves so prevalent in the summer are no longer available, a mixed leaf salad takes on an entirely different character. The winter leaves such as those belonging to the chicory family, endive (both the curly leaved and the Batavian broad-leaf varieties), cabbage leaves, kale, spinach and chard, salad burnet, lamb's lettuce, watercress, Chinese leaves and other imported varieties of lettuce, offer not only a distinctly different taste but in many cases a much heavier crunchy texture. I generally use two or three different varieties of salad leaf, allowing a total weight of approximately 200 g (7 oz) for a side salad for four people. I also choose a dressing which is slightly more robust such as the Spicy mustard dressing. One of my favourite winter combinations uses spinach, chicory and Chinese cabbage.

This salad is also excellent with the addition of pieces of crisply fried bacon and large cubes of avocado pear, when it makes a substantial main course or snack salad.

———

Remove the central stalk from the spinach if necessary and carefully wash and dry. Tear into pieces if too large and put into a big salad bowl.

Trim the hard end of the chicory, slice the head through its length and separate the leaves.

Remove any damaged leaves from the Chinese cabbage and tear into pieces.

Put all the leaves into a big bowl and add the onion. Sprinkle the dressing over the leaves and toss lightly. Serve immediately on individual salad plates.

INGREDIENTS

75 g (3 oz) young spinach leaves
1 small head of chicory
50 g (2 oz) Chinese cabbage
A small piece of onion, peeled and finely sliced
2 tablespoons Spicy mustard dressing (p. 80)

CURRIED PASTA SALAD

S E R V E S

—— 4 - 5 ——

INGREDIENTS

50 g (2 oz) pasta shells
50 g (2 oz) pasta bows,
spirals, or other
interesting shapes
65 ml (2½ fl oz) curried
mayonnaise (p. 103)
25 g (1 oz) raisins
1 small firm eating apple,
cored and roughly
chopped
1 tablespoon lemon juice
3 tablespoons fresh
coriander, finely chopped
A few coriander leaves to
garnish

Rich home-made mayonnaise with a slight hint of curry combines beautifully with the interesting shapes of pasta shells, bows or spirals and the crunchy texture of an apple to give both a smooth and textured result.

Bring a large pan of salted water to the boil and add the pasta. Return to the boil and cook for approximately 10 minutes until the pasta is *al dente* (just tender). Drain and put into a salad bowl with the curried mayonnaise while still hot, tossing lightly to combine. Stir in the raisins and leave until cold.

Mix the apple with the lemon juice and add with the fresh coriander, turning them through the pasta to coat them lightly with the mayonnaise. Scatter a few leaves of coriander on top and serve chilled.

PASTA WITH PESTO SALAD

SERVES
— 4 —

Pesto is a sauce made from fresh basil leaves, olive oil, pine nuts and parmesan cheese. It is one of the most delicious creations, perfectly designed to go with pasta and tomatoes and particularly popular in northern Italy and southern France. Fresh basil can now be bought in convenient packs or as plants. Although in this country basil needs to be grown under glass, it makes a perfect windowsill plant giving off its heady scent every time it is touched, and ensuring a continuous fresh supply.

Pesto sauce is also available fresh or in jars. Commercially prepared pesto can be thinned out to the desired consistency with olive oil before use.

Prepare the pesto sauce by processing all the ingredients in a food processor. The sauce should be thick but not stiff. Add a little extra oil if necessary.

Cook the pasta in a large saucepan of boiling salted water for 6–10 minutes depending on the type being used (see p. 20). Drain and turn into a large salad bowl. Pour on the pesto sauce and toss gently to combine. Leave until cold, then add the tomato halves and toss lightly once again. Serve chilled.

INGREDIENTS

FOR THE PESTO SAUCE
To make about 250 ml (8 fl oz)
6 tablespoons chopped, fresh basil leaves, about 20 g (¾ oz)
1 large clove garlic, peeled and crushed
50 g (2 oz) pine nuts
25 g (1 oz) parmesan cheese
Juice of 1 lemon
150 ml (5 fl oz) olive oil

225 g (8 oz) small pasta shells, shapes or macaroni
8–10 cherry tomatoes, halved

GREEN RICE SALAD

SERVES

—— 6 - 8 ——

100 g (4 oz) long-grain
  patna rice
1 small green pepper, de-
  seeded and chopped into
  5 mm (¼ inch) pieces
1 × 5 cm (2 inch) piece of
  cucumber, cubed
25 g (1 oz) pistachio nuts
25 g (1 oz) currants
A pinch of ground
  cinnamon
Salt and freshly ground
  black pepper
3 tablespoons vinaigrette
  dressing

Although called 'green rice salad', the rice itself is not green, only the ingredients that are included with it – green peppers and pistachio nuts. It makes an excellent salad for a cold buffet, particularly when served along with a selection of lighter leafier salads.

Generally when rice is served as an accompanying dish 50 g (2 oz) per person are allowed; however, when served as part of a salad table with perhaps two or three other salads, I have found that 15 g (½ oz) of rice is sufficient. If the rice has to play a more major role then allow 25 g (1 oz) per person.

Cook the rice uncovered in a large pan of boiling salted water for 11 minutes exactly. Drain and refresh under cold running water until completely cold. Line a baking tin with absorbent kitchen paper and spread the rice on this to dry, covering it also with absorbent paper. When all the moisture has been absorbed by the paper, remove it and turn all the dried rice into a large mixing bowl.

Mix the chopped pepper and cucumber into the rice.

Peel the skin from the pistachio nuts by covering with boiling water for a few minutes until the skins can be easily pressed off. Drain and refresh in cold water to set their green colour before removing the skins. Cut in slivers and add to the rice and peppers.

Finally, stir in the currants, cinnamon and seasoning to taste, along with the vinaigrette dressing to moisten, and serve chilled.

BROWN RICE & BEAN SALAD

SERVES

— 8 —

The 'nutty' flavour of wholegrain rice and the strong sweet flavour of the small dark red adzuki bean have been combined together for many thousands of years in the soups, salads and savoury dishes of the Far East. In this salad I have also included French beans which makes this a highly textured and colourful salad. Because of the small quantities of ingredients used it is not worth making less than eight portions of this salad. However, it will keep well in the refrigerator for several days.

Put the adzuki beans and their soaking water into a saucepan, bring to the boil and cook for 50 minutes–1 hour until tender.

Put the rice in a large saucepan of boiling water and cook uncovered for 20–25 minutes until just tender.

Cook the French beans in a large pot of boiling water for 5 minutes until just tender. Drain and refresh under cold running water until cold.

While both the beans and the rice are cooking, prepare the other vegetable ingredients and make the dressing by combining all the ingredients in a screw-top jar and shaking until well blended.

When the beans and rice are cooked, drain well and turn into a large bowl. Pour on the dressing and mix lightly to coat. Leave until cold before adding the French beans, pepper, celery and onions. Season to taste with salt and pepper, if required, sprinkle with coriander and serve chilled.

INGREDIENTS

FOR THE SALAD

50 g (2 oz) adzuki beans, soaked overnight

100 g (4 oz) wholegrain or brown rice

100 g (4 oz) fresh French green beans, cut in 2 cm (¾ inch) lengths

1 small green pepper, de-seeded and chopped

2 sticks celery, finely chopped

3 spring onions, finely chopped

Salt and freshly ground black pepper

3 tablespoons fresh coriander leaves, finely chopped, to garnish

FOR THE DRESSING

1 teaspoon Dijon mustard

9 tablespoons olive oil

3 tablespoons red wine vinegar

2 cloves garlic, peeled and crushed

Salt and freshly ground black pepper

1 teaspoon tamari sauce

45

CRACKED WHEAT SALAD

SERVES

— 4 —

75 g (3 oz) cracked wheat
25 g (1 oz) flat-leaved parsley, finely chopped
3 large sprigs of mint, finely chopped
4 spring onions, finely chopped
2–3 cloves garlic, peeled and crushed
175 g (6 oz) tomatoes, finely chopped
Juice of 1 lemon
2 tablespoons olive oil
Salt and freshly ground black pepper

Cracked wheat, also called burgul and bulgar wheat, is obtained by boiling and drying the grains before grinding. It is one of the staple foods of the Middle East and features in the Lebanese salad Tabbouleh. In recent years since bulgar wheat has become more readily available in this country it has become more popular. The predominant flavours should be mint, garlic, lemon and parsley. It is very quick and easy to make and is delicious as part of a collection of salads or served with crisp salad leaves such as Cos (Romaine) or 'Little Gem' hearts, tomatoes and green peppers.

Cover the cracked wheat in cold water and soak for about 20–30 minutes; turn into a sieve and press out all the water. The wheat will have swollen, become tender and edible.

Combine the remaining ingredients in a large salad bowl and stir in the cracked wheat. Season to taste, cover and leave in the refrigerator for at least 15 minutes before serving.

BUTTER BEAN & ANCHOVY SALAD

S E R V E S

—— 4 ——

Butter or lima beans are kidney-shaped beans, pale green or cream in colour. They come in a variety of sizes and retain their shape well when cooked, which makes them valuable as a salad vegetable. They have a meaty texture which absorbs other flavours well. The anchovy fillets can be soaked for 30 minutes in milk to remove the excess salt if necessary.

225 g (8 oz) dried butter beans, soaked overnight, or 1 × 300 g (11 oz) tin of cooked butter beans
2 celery stalks, cut into 3 mm (⅛ inch) pieces
1 × 7.5 cm (3 inch) piece cucumber
1 × 50 g (2 oz) can anchovy fillets, drained
4 tablespoons vinaigrette dressing (p. 95)

If using soaked, dried beans, drain and boil in fresh water for 30–40 minutes, boiling fast for the first 10 minutes. Drain and refresh under cold running water until completely cold. If using canned beans, drain. Put the beans in a large mixing bowl.

Cut the cucumber in half widthways and slice each half into 5 mm (¼ inch) sticks. Add to the beans with the drained anchovy fillets.

Pour the vinaigrette dressing over and toss lightly to coat. Serve chilled.

47

GREEN BEAN SALAD

S E R V E S

—— 4 - 5 ——

INGREDIENTS

*75 g (3 oz) chick peas,
   soaked overnight*
75 g (3 oz) French beans
*50 g (2 oz) walnuts,
   halved*
*2 spring onions, trimmed
   and finely chopped*
*8 black olives, stoned and
   halved*
*25 ml (1 fl oz) Piquant
   dressing (p. 98)*
*2 tablespoons parsley,
   finely chopped*
*Salt and freshly ground
   black pepper*

Green beans, native to South America, embrace many different varieties such as French beans (often referred to as green haricot beans, haricots verts, or thin green string beans) and runner beans, a coarser, thicker variety of bean with a less delicate flavour. They are both available in fully grown and dwarf varieties. Green beans make a deliciously crunchy salad, whether raw or lightly cooked, alone or in combination either together or with dried beans, to give a varied shape, taste and texture.

If using dried soaked chick peas, drain and boil in fresh water for 1 hour 10 minutes, boiling fast for the first 10 minutes. If using canned beans, drain. Put the drained beans into a salad bowl.

Top and tail the green beans and cook in boiling water for 3–4 minutes, drain in a colander and refresh under cold running water until completely cold. This will stop the cooking, set the colour and ensure that the beans retain their crisp texture and fresh flavour. Cut each bean in half and add to the chick peas along with the walnut halves, spring onions and olives.

Pour over the dressing, and toss lightly to coat the vegetables. Add the parsley, season to taste. Toss lightly and serve well chilled.

COLESLAW

S E R V E S

—— 4 ——

No matter how simple or sophisticated the occasion, coleslaw is the one salad which is always a success. Originally from America, this salad derives its name from the Dutch *koolsla* meaning cabbage salad. The basis of the salad is traditionally, therefore, the firm white 'Dutch' cabbage, and although many other vegetables are often added and indeed substituted for it, the true coleslaw is a salad of finely shredded cabbage steeped in mayonnaise. The cabbage can be cut very finely by hand or shredded in a food processor using a fine slicing blade to give long slivers of cabbage rather than short stumpy pieces.

Mix the mayonnaise and black pepper in a large bowl. Divide the cabbage in half, and cut out the core. Shred very finely into the bowl with the mayonnaise and toss well to coat.

Add the carrot, onion, half the parsley and toss again to combine all the ingredients. Season to taste, cover and chill for 1 hour before serving.

If the salad exudes an excess of liquid, which it may do if the carrot is very juicy, drain away and toss the salad again adding a little more mayonnaise if necessary.

Turn into a salad bowl. Sprinkle with the remaining parsley and paprika pepper.

Coleslaw will keep in the refrigerator for one or two days. After this time it becomes very wet and loses its texture.

INGREDIENTS

150 ml (5 fl oz) thick mayonnaise (p. 100)
Freshly ground black pepper
225 g (8 oz) white hard-headed cabbage
1 carrot, approximately 50 g (2 oz), grated
25 g (1 oz) onion, peeled and finely chopped
2 tablespoons parsley, finely chopped
¼ teaspoon paprika pepper

CURRIED COLESLAW

S E R V E S

— 4 —

INGREDIENTS

150 ml (5 fl oz) Curried
mayonnaise (p. 101)
1 tablespoon mango
chutney
Freshly ground black
pepper
½ small white hard-headed
cabbage, approximately
225 g (8 oz)
25 g (1 oz) onion, peeled
and finely chopped
1 small carrot,
approximately 50 g
(2 oz), grated
2 tablespoons parsley,
finely chopped
50 g (2 oz) sultanas or
raisins
50 g (2 oz) unsalted
peanuts
¼ teaspoon paprika pepper

This popular version of the traditional coleslaw uses a curried mayonnaise to dress the shredded cabbage and grated carrot with the addition of raisins and nuts for added taste and texture.

Mix the mayonnaise, mango chutney and pepper in a large bowl. Divide the cabbage in half and cut out the core. Shred very finely into the bowl with the mayonnaise and toss well to coat.

Add the onion, carrot, half the parsley, sultanas and peanuts and toss again to combine all the ingredients. Season to taste, cover and chill for 1 hour before transferring to a salad bowl and sprinkling with the remaining parsley and paprika pepper.

NUTTY COLESLAW

S E R V E S
—— 4 - 6 ——

With a base of inexpensive ingredients such as cabbage and carrot (in season of course) this salad can afford to have a few more luxurious ingredients added such as peppers, beans and nuts, to create a crunchy salad with an interesting texture and colour. Moistened with a light mayonnaise it makes an excellent salad for a cold table. It can also be made using a citrus dressing (p. 96)

Combine the mayonnaise, pepper and apple in a large mixing bowl. Divide the cabbage in half and cut out the core. Shred very finely into the bowl with the carrot and toss, to moisten in the dressing. Add the peppers, beans, nuts and half the parsley. Toss well to combine all the ingredients and coat in the dressing. Transfer to a salad bowl, sprinkle with the remaining parsley and serve chilled.

INGREDIENTS

150 ml (5 fl oz)
    mayonnaise (p. 100)
Freshly ground black
    pepper
1 red apple, diced
225 g (8 oz) white hard-
    headed cabbage
1 carrot, approximately
    100 g (4 oz), grated
1 small red and 1 small
    green pepper,
    approximately 100 g
    (4 oz) each, de-seeded
    and chopped into 5 mm
    (¼ inch) pieces
50 g (2 oz) French 'bobby'
    beans, topped, tailed and
    halved
50–100 g (2–4 oz)
    walnuts, pecan nuts,
    brazil nuts or unsalted
    peanuts, roughly
    chopped
2 tablespoons parsley,
    finely chopped

ELEGANT COLESLAW

S E R V E S
—— 4 - 6 ——

*150 ml (5 fl oz) thick
    mayonnaise (p. 100)*
¼ teaspoon cayenne pepper
1 teaspoon fennel seeds
1 teaspoon caraway seeds
*Freshly ground black
    pepper*
*100 g (4 oz) white hard-
    headed cabbage*
*100 g (4 oz) red hard-
    headed cabbage*
*1 small carrot,
    approximately 50 g
    (2 oz), grated*
*25 g (1 oz) onion, peeled
    and finely chopped*
1 celery stalk, finely sliced
1 small red pepper, diced
50 g (2 oz) raisins
1 tablespoon pumpkin seeds

This colourful variation on the traditional coleslaw is as its name implies an 'elegant' mélange of finely chopped ingredients. Hard-headed white Dutch cabbage is mixed with similarly hard-headed red cabbage and the texture and colour further heightened with the addition of celery and red pepper. The mayonnaise too is spiked with fennel and caraway seed and a dusting of cayenne pepper. The result is delicious.

Mix the mayonnaise with the cayenne pepper, fennel and caraway seeds and black pepper in a large mixing bowl.

Divide the cabbages in half and cut out the cores. Shred finely into the bowl and toss lightly to combine and coat.

Add the carrot, onion, celery, pepper and raisins and toss again to mix well. Season to taste.

Cover and chill for 1 hour before turning into a salad bowl. Sprinkle with the pumpkin seeds before serving.

WINTER SALAD

S E R V E S

—— 4 - 6 ——

This salad is a type of coleslaw in that it combines shredded, grated and chopped vegetables in a moist dressing. The difference, however, is that Brussels sprouts are used instead of cabbage which not only gives variety to the salad table but is an excellent way of using up the larger Brussels sprouts. The dressing is also lighter to match the texture of the salad ingredients, but has an interesting sharp spicy flavour.

Combine the yoghurt, mayonnaise, mustard and seasoning in a large bowl and beat well to combine.

Discard any tough outer leaves from the Brussels sprouts, trim the bases and wash and dry well. Finely shred the sprouts either by hand or in a food processor.

Add to the dressing mixture along with the carrots, celery and walnuts. Toss well to combine and coat in the dressing. Season to taste adding extra if necessary.

Turn into a salad bowl, sprinkle with sunflower seeds, cover and chill until ready to serve.

INGREDIENTS

150 ml (5 fl oz) natural yoghurt
65 ml (2½ fl oz) thick mayonnaise (p. 100)
½ teaspoon Meaux or wholegrain mustard
Pinch salt and freshly ground black pepper
450 g (1 lb) Brussels sprouts
225 g (8 oz) carrots, grated
4 celery stalks, finely sliced
25–50 g (1–2 oz) walnuts, broken
1 tablespoon sunflower seeds

CARROT & NUT SALAD

SERVES
— 4 —

INGREDIENTS

225 g (8 oz) carrots, grated
1 × 198 g (7 oz) can
  sweetcorn kernels,
  drained
40 g (1½ oz) sultanas
50 g (2 oz) peanuts or
  cashew nuts
5 tablespoons vinaigrette
  dressing (p. 95)
Freshly ground black
  pepper

One of the most popular salads both in my restaurant and catering company is a simple combination of grated carrots, sweetcorn and nuts moistened with a well flavoured vinaigrette dressing. Any type of nuts already in stock will do, but for this particular salad I favour cashews, or unsalted peanuts. The quantity of dressing used may also vary depending on the moistness of the carrots. Use just enough to coat and flavour the ingredients without destroying their crisp texture or making them soggy.

Combine the carrots, sweetcorn, sultanas and nuts in a large bowl and toss to mix evenly. Pour on enough dressing to lightly coat and moisten. Season to taste. Transfer to a salad bowl, cover and chill until required.

CAULIFLOWER & BEAN SALAD

S E R V E S

—— 4 - 8 ——

The combination of fresh tight-headed cauliflower flor-ets, finely shredded cabbage and grated carrot, amal-gamates well with the softer texture of red kidney beans and sweetcorn to make this a colourful and nutritious salad. I sometimes also use green broccoli, calabrese florets with or instead of the cauliflower. Because of the ingredients used in this salad, it is not worth making a small quantity.

———

Divide the cabbage in half and cut out the core. Combine in a large mixing bowl with the cauliflower, carrot, sweetcorn and kidney beans. Season with pepper and herbs and toss well to combine.

Pour over the vinaigrette dressing and toss again. Season to taste and adjust if necessary. Cover and store in the refrigerator for 1 hour to develop the flavours. Transfer to a salad bowl and serve.

INGREDIENTS

50 g (2 oz) white hard-
  headed cabbage
100 g (4 oz) cauliflower
  florets
50 g (2 oz) carrot, grated
1 × 198 g (7 oz) can
  sweetcorn kernels,
  drained
1 × 213 g (5.51 oz) can
  red kidney beans,
  drained
Freshly ground black
  pepper
2 tablespoons fresh
  coriander or parsley,
  finely chopped
3 tablespoons vinaigrette
  dressing

MUSHROOM, MUNG BEAN & RED PEPPER SALAD

SERVES

—— 4 ——

INGREDIENTS

1 clove garlic, peeled and crushed

100 ml (3½ fl oz) natural yoghurt

2 tablespoons lemon juice

100 g (4 oz) white button mushrooms

50 g (2 oz) mung bean sprouts

1 tablespoon snipped chives

1 small red pepper, de-seeded and cut into 3 mm × 4 cm (⅛ × 1½ inch) slivers

Freshly ground black pepper

1 teaspoon paprika pepper

Watercress leaves to garnish

Tiny, white, firm-fleshed mushrooms, although not with quite the meaty, earthy flavour of field mushrooms, do have a certain delicate taste and crisp texture which lends itself particularly well to raw salad dishes. This one combines sprouted mung beans (p. 108) with slivers of red pepper and is coated in a garlic, lemon and yoghurt dressing, served garnished with watercress leaves.

Place the garlic, yoghurt and lemon juice in a bowl and beat to combine.

Wipe and slice the mushrooms and add to the dressing with the mung beans, chives and pepper. Toss lightly in the dressing to combine, so that all the vegetables have a light coating.

Pile into a salad bowl, sprinkle with black and paprika pepper and garnish with watercress leaves.

This salad needs to be eaten on the day of making as it loses its attractive colour, texture and appearance if kept too long.

CRUNCHY
CUCUMBER SALAD

S E R V E S
—— 4 ——

This refreshing salad of chunky pieces of cucumber, spring onions and tofu (soya bean curd) makes an excellent side salad, particularly when served with a spicy meat dish such as Chicken and beef satay salad (p. 83).

Divide the lettuce hearts into individual leaves, wash and dry well. Place in a salad bowl.

Cut the cucumber in half lengthwise, then in slices about 5 mm (¼ inch) thick. Add to the bowl with the lettuce.

Cut the spring onions into 2.5 cm (1 inch) lengths and then into fine sticks and also add to the bowl. Toss all the ingredients together lightly.

Cut the tofu into 1 cm (½ inch) cubes and arrange through the salad. Do not toss it because it is quite fragile. Sprinkle with the coriander or parsley and serve.

INGREDIENTS

2 'Little Gem' lettuce
   hearts
225 g (8 oz) piece of
   cucumber
4 spring onions, white and
   green
½ × 148 g (5.25 oz)
   carton silken tofu
2 tablespoons chopped,
   fresh coriander or parsley

CHINESE SALAD

SERVES

—— 4 ——

50 g (2 oz) mange-tout peas

100 g (4 oz) Chinese cabbage, shredded finely

2 spring onions, white and green, cut into 4 cm (1½ inch) pieces

25 g (1 oz) button mushrooms, sliced

50 g (2 oz) red pepper, de-seeded and cut into 3 mm × 4.5 cm (⅛ × 1¾ inch) strips

6 whole baby sweetcorn

50 g (2 oz) mung bean sprouts

½ tablespoon sesame seeds, toasted

2–3 tablespoons Oriental dressing (p. 98)

In this salad, a selection of fresh crisp vegetables, including bean sprouts, sweetcorn and Chinese cabbage, are combined in a spicy oriental dressing. The fresh flavour, colour and texture of this salad makes it the perfect accompaniment to many main dishes, particularly highly spiced meat and vegetarian dishes made from nuts, seeds and lentils.

Top and tail the mange-tout peas and cut in half diagonally across their width if necessary. Combine all the vegetables and seeds in a bowl and toss gently to mix.

Pour the oriental dressing over and toss again to coat the vegetables. Transfer to a salad bowl and serve immediately.

This salad will keep no longer than a day as the delicate vegetables, like those used in a green salad, wilt easily once dressed. However, all the vegetables can be prepared and combined several hours before use, covered and stored in the refrigerator, to be dressed just before serving.

CURRIED VEGETABLE SALAD

SERVES

— 4 —

Vegetables are one of the most colourful, interesting and inspiring collections of food. With them all kinds of wonderfully healthy and tasty dishes can be created to tempt the palate and comfort the soul. This combination of crunchy raw vegetables dressed in a curried French dressing is one of the many creations possible. Use a little thought, imagination and courage to create a few for yourself.

Put the vinaigrette dressing, coriander, curry paste or powder, and turmeric in a large mixing bowl and whisk well to blend.

Trim off any tender green young leaves surrounding the cauliflower head and shred finely. Discard the stalk and break the head into florets. Add to the dressing with the carrot, celery, courgette, onion and sultanas.

Toss well to combine and season to taste. Cover and chill for an hour to allow the flavours to develop before turning into a salad bowl. Sprinkle with the sesame seeds and fresh coriander before serving.

INGREDIENTS

100 ml (3½ fl oz) vinaigrette dressing (p. 95)
1 teaspoon ground coriander
1 teaspoon curry paste or powder
1 teaspoon turmeric
175 g (6 oz) cauliflower (trimmed weight)
1 small carrot, approximately 50 g (2 oz), grated
3 celery stalks, sliced
1 small courgette, approximately 50 g (2 oz), sliced in rings
50 g (2 oz) onion, peeled and finely chopped
50 g (2 oz) sultanas
1 teaspoon sesame seeds
2 tablespoons chopped fresh coriander

POTATO SALAD

Almost every country in the world has its own variation on potato salad. Some are quite simple, to be used as accompaniments; others are mixed with all sorts of ingredients such as diced sausage, bacon, raw smoked ham, anchovies, eggs, pickled and other vegetables, which make them more substantial.

The secret of a good potato salad, as with all cooking, is to use the correct ingredients of the best quality. A waxy potato is best because it will hold its shape both in cooking and mixing. If they are new, small and of even size, they are best just scrubbed and left whole. If old and irregular in form, they can be cut into slices or cubes. They can be cooked with a few sprigs of mint. Cutting the potatoes is done before cooking commercially, but for small quantities I prefer to slice or cube the potatoes after they have been cooked.

The dressing too, whether vinaigrette or mayonnaise, must be of good quality. There are a number of excellent commercial brands available which are very useful in emergencies, however none can quite match those that are home-made.

The method of making the salad is also important and over the years I have achieved the best results by coating the potatoes in their dressing while they are still warm. This enables them to absorb the flavour while giving them a protective covering which helps retain their colour. When making potato mayonnaise I sometimes toss the potatoes in a little vinaigrette (p. 95) while they are still warm, then coat in the mayonnaise (p. 100) when cold.

Depending on the taste I require I might add a very finely chopped shallot or small onion to the hot potatoes, or spinkle with finely snipped chives when the dressed salad is cold. For special occasions I use halved pickled walnuts to decorate the edge of the salad bowl and sprinkle the potatoes with paprika pepper. Potatoes in vinaigrette make a lighter salad in taste and texture. Add some chopped spring onions and season with freshly ground black pepper and chopped herbs such as chervil, mint, parsley and chives.

POTATO MAYONNAISE

S E R V E S

—— 4 - 6 ——

New baby potatoes or diced or sliced potatoes are coated in a thick mayonnaise and flavoured and garnished with chives.

1 kg (2 lb) small new
  potatoes
2 sprigs of mint
1 teaspoon salt
4 tablespoons vinaigrette
  (p. 95)
250 ml (8 fl oz) thick
  mayonnaise (p. 100)
3–4 tablespoons snipped
  chives

Wash and scrub the potatoes and place in a large saucepan of boiling water with the mint and salt. Return to the boil, cover and simmer for 15–20 minutes until just tender, in order to keep their shape. Drain in a colander. The potatoes can also be steamed.

Place the warm potatoes in a large bowl and gently toss in the vinaigrette. Add the mayonnaise and continue to toss until the potatoes are well coated. Hands are the most satisfactory way of doing the tossing. Allow to cool before adding the chives and turning into a salad bowl. Potato mayonnaise is best eaten fresh, but will keep quite well for a day in the refrigerator.

For curried potato mayonnaise substitute the traditional mayonnaise for curried mayonnaise (p. 101).

POLISH POTATO SALAD

SERVES

—— 4 - 6 ——

INGREDIENTS

1 kg (2 lb) small new
  potatoes
1 teaspoon salt
2 tablespoons white wine
1 small beetroot, 50–75 g
  (2–3 oz), cooked, peeled
  and finely grated
1 tablespoon horseradish
  sauce
3 tablespoons mayonnaise
  (p. 100)
A pinch of mustard powder
100 ml (3½ fl oz) natural
  yoghurt
Freshly ground black
  pepper
1 tablespoon snipped chives

I frequently enjoyed this colourful salad at the home of a friend whose family were Polish. She kindly gave me the recipe. This salad looks particularly attractive with a border of crisp salad leaves, garnished with a few shreds of radicchio leaves.

Cook the potatoes in boiling salted water until just tender, in order to keep their shape. Drain in a colander. Place the warm potatoes into a large bowl and pour on the white wine, tossing to coat. Allow to cool.

Add the beetroot, horseradish, mayonnaise and mustard powder, stirring well to combine. Stir in the natural yoghurt and season to taste. Pour over the potatoes, toss lightly to coat and serve sprinkled with chives. This salad will keep well for one day if covered and stored in the refrigerator.

MUSTARD & DILL POTATO SALAD

SERVES
— 4 —

This potato salad is mixed with celery, dill pickles and red onions before being coated in a light mustard and dill dressing and garnished with snipped chives.

Cook the potatoes in boiling salted water until just tender, in order to keep their shape. Drain in a colander and leave to cool.

Combine the dill pickles, celery and onion in a large bowl and add the cold potatoes.

Mix the mustard, mayonnaise and soured cream together and season with pepper and dill. Pour over the potato and vegetable mixture and toss lightly to coat. Transfer to a salad bowl and sprinkle with the chives. This will keep well in the refrigerator for up to two days.

INGREDIENTS

1 kg (2 lb) small new
    potatoes
1 teaspoon salt
2 dill pickles, halved and
    cut into thin strips
3 celery stalks, thinly sliced
1 small red-skinned onion,
    approximately 100 g
    (4 oz), thinly sliced
2 tablespoons Dijon
    mustard
5 tablespoons mayonnaise
    (p. 100)
65 ml (2½ fl oz) soured
    cream
Freshly ground black
    pepper
2 tablespoons dill, finely
    chopped or 1 tablespoon
    dried dill
2 tablespoons chives,
    snipped in 2 cm (¾ in)
    lengths

RUSSIAN SALAD

S E R V E S

—— 4 ——

*225 g (8 oz) beetroot,
cooked, peeled and diced*

*50 g (2 oz) carrot, diced
and cooked*

*50 g (2 oz) potato, diced
and cooked*

*1 celery stalk, diced and
cooked*

3 tablespoons peas, cooked

*3 tablespoons vinaigrette
(p. 95)*

*3 tablespoons mayonnaise
(p. 100)*

*Freshly ground black
pepper*

1 tablespoon snipped chives

Memories of Russian salad are of tasteless frozen vegetables drowned in a watery mayonnaise, or unappetising cans of mixed vegetable salad, reminiscent of student flats and hotel kitchens. I felt inspired to create a Russian salad considerably more delicious. It can be made using vegetables cooked specifically for the salad, or pre-cooked vegetables such as the fresh beetroot available in vacuum packs in most shops. It is an excellent way of using up left-over vegetables – particularly for a quick and easy salad. The vegetables should be cut into 5 mm (¼ in) dice and, in true Russian tradition, the combined amount of vegetables should be just half the quantity of the beetroot.

Combine the cooked vegetables in a large bowl and mix together. Pour over vinaigrette. If using cold vegetables, heat the vinaigrette and pour while warm over the vegetables. Leave to cool. Add the mayonnaise and pepper and toss to coat the vegetables. Transfer to a salad bowl, and sprinkle with the chives. This salad will keep for up to two days in the refrigerator.

Page 67 : CHINESE SALAD (PAGE 58)

Page 68 : CURRIED COLESLAW (PAGE 50); ELEGANT COLESLAW
(PAGE 52) AND NUTTY COLESLAW (PAGE 51)

SWEET & SOUR COURGETTES

SERVES

—— 4 ——

This wonderfully tasty, lightly cooked salad with its perfect balance of sweet and sour, is particularly good when made with whole tiny tender young courgettes. However, the dish can be made with medium size vegetables and is an excellent way of using them at the height of their season when there is a glut.

———

Heat half the oil in a large frying pan and fry the garlic and the courgette pieces, in batches, until they are lightly golden on each side. Remove from the pan with a draining spoon, dry well on kitchen paper and place into a mixing bowl. Add more oil when necessary.

Combine all the ingredients for the sweet and sour dressing in a screw-top jar and shake well to blend. Pour over the hot courgettes, toss lightly to coat in the dressing and transfer to a salad bowl. Serve well chilled.

INGREDIENTS

FOR THE SALAD
25 ml (1 fl oz) olive or
  sunflower oil
2 cloves garlic, peeled and
  crushed
4–6 courgettes,
  approximately 450 g
  (1 lb), cut into 2 cm
  (¾ inch) slices

**FOR THE SWEET AND
SOUR DRESSING**
4 tablespoons soy sauce
4 tablespoons lemon juice
1 tablespoon cider or wine
  vinegar
2 tablespoons liquid honey
Salt and freshly ground
  black pepper

Page 70 : CHICKEN AND PINEAPPLE SALAD (PAGE 82)

Page 69 : ALTERNATIVE CAESAR SALAD (PAGE 74)

VEGETABLES A LA GRECQUE

SERVES
—— 4 ——

This is one of the traditional French ways of preparing vegetables to be served cold. It preserves their colour, flavour and texture, and looks most attractive as well as tasting delicious. A selection of three or four vegetables can be prepared in this way, either on their own or in combination. Keep the quantities of each roughly the same, allowing 750 g (1½ lb) in total. They are gently stewed in an aromatic liquid of olive oil, water, white wine, lemon juice and herbs. The vegetables which take longest to cook are added to the liquid first so that when the dish is complete all the vegetables will have the same crisp, firm texture. Vegetables à la greçque will keep well for several days in the refrigerator.

―――

Prepare the marinade by combining all the ingredients in a large casserole and bringing to the boil. Simmer for 10–15 minutes to combine the flavours.

Meanwhile prepare the vegetables. Peel the button onions by plunging into boiling water for 1 minute; drain and remove the skins (they will now strip away easily). Trim the roots and stems of the onions carefully to prevent them from falling apart during the cooking. Trim the top of the fennel, reserving the feathery fronds for garnish, and cut the bulb into eight pieces through its length. Break the cauliflower head into florets about the size of a cherry tomato. Wipe the mushrooms and trim the stems level with the caps.

Put the onions and fennel into the cooking liquor; return to the boil, then reduce the heat to a very low simmer, cover and cook gently for 5–10 minutes. Add the button mushrooms and cook for a further minute. Pour the vegetables into a colander set over a saucepan to catch the liquid. Remove the seeds and discard the bouquet garni.

Arrange the vegetables in a serving dish and boil the cooking liquid vigorously to reduce to 65 ml (2½ fl oz). Pour over the vegetables. Leave to cool and serve garnished with parsley and fennel fronds.

INGREDIENTS

FOR THE MARINADE
For 750 g (1½ lb) vegetables
450 ml (15 fl oz) water
65 ml (2½ fl oz) dry white wine
65 ml (2½ fl oz) olive oil
Juice of 1 large lemon
2–3 cloves garlic, peeled and crushed
Generous bouquet garni made from parsley stalks, bay leaf, and a sprig of thyme
1 × 10 cm (4 inch) celery stalk
2 teaspoons mustard seeds, crushed
2 teaspoons coriander seeds, crushed
2 teaspoons black peppercorns

FOR THE VEGETABLES
175 g (6 oz) button or pickling onions
1 small bulb fennel, approximately 175 g (6 oz)
175 g (6 oz) cauliflower
175 g (6 oz) button mushrooms
1 tablespoon parsley, finely chopped

Mushrooms à la greçque can be made using the same marinade with the addition of 1 tablespoon each of tomato purée and muscovado sugar. 450 g (1 lb) mushrooms is substituted for the vegetables and these are simmered in the marinade for 2–3 minutes and served sprinkled with parsley.

SPANISH PEPPER SALAD

SERVES

— 4 —

This wonderful Spanish dish of red, yellow and green peppers makes an ideal accompanying salad or a tasty first course. When the peppers are roasted, as in this recipe, they take on a very rich mellow flavour which is truly delicious.

Pre-heat the oven to gas mark 6, 400°F (200°C). Oven time: 40–45 minutes.

Wipe the peppers, cut in half lengthwise and remove the seeds and white pith. Lightly oil a baking try and place the halved peppers on it, skin side down. Bake for about 30 minutes then turn over and continue to cook for a further 10–15 minutes.

Meantime, prepare the marinade by combining all the ingredients in a deep glass or earthenware dish.

When the peppers are cooked, remove from the oven, and place while still hot in a thick polythene bag. Seal and leave for 8–10 minutes before removing from the bag and pressing the skins off with the fingers. Alternatively, the cooked peppers can be sprayed with cold water which also makes peeling easier.

Cut each pepper in half again and place in the dish with the marinade while still warm. Cover and leave overnight for the flavours to develop. Serve chilled with fresh crusty bread and a bowl of black olives. Peppers prepared this way will keep in the refrigerator for several days.

INGREDIENTS

FOR THE SALAD
750 g–1 kg (1½–2 lb)
   mixed red, green and
   yellow peppers, de-
   seeded
1 tablespoon olive oil
2 tablespoons parsley,
   finely chopped

FOR THE MARINADE
2–3 cloves garlic, peeled
   and crushed
A pinch of salt
Finely ground black pepper
50 ml (2 fl oz) white wine
   vinegar
175 ml (6 fl oz) olive oil
1 teaspoon chilli sauce
1 tablespoon chopped, fresh
   oregano

MAIN COURSE SALADS

With the increasing awareness of salad ingredients as important foods in a healthy diet, a much greater demand for a wider range has been created. As a result, salads are no longer relegated to the position of 'extras' or dull alternatives for the slimmer or the vegetarian. Colourful and nourishing composed or main course salads are now becoming just as important on the menu.

Main course salads can be composed entirely of vegetables or they can be combined with meat, poultry, fish or dairy produce. The type of salad served, therefore, will obviously depend on its role. The Greek and Caesar salads on pp. 73 and 74, are excellent examples of simple main course salads, whereas the Chicken and beef satay from Malaya (p. 83) with its spicy peanut sauce, and the Mussel and rice salad on p. 86 are examples of more substantial meals.

Over the years many salad creations have been so well loved that they have become 'classic' dishes; salads such as the famous Salade Niçoise from Provence (p. 84), or Coronation chicken salad (p. 81), are good examples. Other very individual and often unrecognised combinations of salad ingredients will, I hope, provide interesting new additions to your salad repertoire and give you the enthusiasm and courage to create inspired compositions for yourself.

GREEK SALAD

SERVES

— 4 —

This wonderful salad evokes nostalgic memories of Greece, her people, the sun and the sea. The main ingredients are tomatoes, cucumber, spring onions, olives and Feta cheese. This is a sharp-tasting cheese made from ewe's or goat's milk, which can be bought in cans or sealed packets. In both cases it has a long shelf life, but once opened will keep in the refrigerator for several days.

───────

Lay the lettuce leaves on top of each other, roll up and slice thinly across the roll. Scatter over one large or individual serving dishes.

Arrange the tomatoes and cucumber on top of the lettuce in overlapping slices, leaving a good lettuce rim round the edge of the plate and scatter the onion on top.

Mix the oil and lemon juice together and drizzle over the salad. Freshly grind black pepper over the tomatoes and cucumber and arrange the Feta cubes and olives on top.

Scatter the fresh oregano over the salad and serve immediately with pitta bread.

INGREDIENTS

100 g (4 oz) crisp lettuce leaves
4 sweet red tomatoes, sliced
¼ cucumber, sliced thinly
2–4 spring onions, finely sliced
3 tablespoons olive oil
1–2 tablespoons lemon juice
Freshly ground black pepper
100 g (4 oz) feta cheese, cubed
12 stoned black olives
2 tablespoons oregano, roughly chopped

CAESAR SALAD

S E R V E S
—— 4 ——

INGREDIENTS

2 large heads Cos or
  'Romaine' lettuce
2 eggs
6 tablespoons olive oil
Salt and freshly ground
  black pepper
Juice of 1 lemon
1 teaspoon Worcestershire
  sauce
25 g (1 oz) Parmesan
  cheese
75 g (3 oz) white garlic
  croûtons (p. 110)

This famous American salad was created by Caesar Cardini during the 1920s when he had a restaurant in Mexico. Since then it has been adopted by chefs throughout the world and today there are innumerable versions. Traditionally however, the main ingredients are Cos lettuce hearts, fine olive oil, lemons, salt, pepper, Worcestershire sauce, fresh Parmesan cheese, garlic-flavoured croûtons and a very lightly boiled egg – no anchovies as many recipes state.

The success of the salad is in its tossing and mixing which should be gentle enough to coat but not bruise the leaves. Traditionally, the salad was eaten with the fingers, the lettuce leaves being used to scoop up the sauce and croûtons. This salad can be served as a first course but the quantities given below are sufficient for a light main course.

Strip the lettuce leaves carefully from the stalk and select about 20–24 whole leaves from the heart of the lettuce, no more than 15 cms (6 inches) long. Save the remaining leaves for another salad. Wash and dry the selected leaves and place in a plastic bag in the refrigerator until required.

Collect all the ingredients together just before serving. Boil the eggs for exactly 1 minute then plunge into cold water to stop the cooking. Pour the oil in a large salad bowl, add the lettuce and toss well, taking care not to break the leaves. Sprinkle with the salt and freshly ground black pepper. Toss again. Drizzle over the lemon juice and Worcestershire sauce. Break the eggs on top, scraping out the thin layer of cooked white near the shell. Toss again, then sprinkle on the cheese and croûtons and give a final toss. Arrange the salad on large plates and serve immediately.

NOTE

ALTERNATIVE CAESAR SALAD
For those who may be concerned about eating raw eggs, or simply prefer them cooked, follow the same recipe, above, but instead hard boil the eggs, cut into quarters and toss into the ingredients. This recipe is equally delicious although not entirely traditional. (See p 69).

ORIENTAL SALAD

S E R V E S

—— 4 ——

This light, refreshing salad based on crisp Chinese leaves, also known as Chinese or Shantung cabbage, makes a delightful accompanying salad. A mixed variety of sprouted beans, bamboo shoots, water chestnuts, green pepper and spring onions combine with the lettuce to be tossed in a light soya sauce dressing.

Pull the washed and dried Chinese leaves apart and shred finely. Pick over the bean sprouts; wash and dry thoroughly. Put all the ingredients in a large salad bowl and toss lightly to combine.

Prepare the dressing by combining the ingredients in a screw-top jar; shake to emulsify. Just before serving pour over the salad and toss lightly to coat. Serve immediately.

INGREDIENTS

FOR THE SALAD
1 head Chinese leaves, approximately 375 g (13 oz)
100–175 g (4–6 oz) fresh bean sprouts (p. 108)
1 × 227 g (8 oz) tin of water chestnuts, drained and sliced
1 × 227 g (8 oz) tin of bamboo shoots, drained and sliced
1 large green pepper, de-seeded and cut into 3 mm × 5 cm (⅛ × 2 inch) strips
6 spring onions, white and green, trimmed and cut into 4–5 cm (1½–2 inch) lengths

FOR THE DRESSING
2 tablespoons olive oil
1 tablespoon sesame oil
1 tablespoon wine vinegar
1 tablespoon soya sauce
Freshly ground black pepper

WEST COAST SALAD

SERVES

—— 4 ——

INGREDIENTS

100 g (4 oz) 'Iceberg'
lettuce leaves
50 g (2 oz) French beans,
topped and tailed and
halved
100 g (4 oz) broccoli
florets
1 small green pepper, de-
seeded and cut into thin
strips
3 celery stalks, cut into
5 mm (¼ inch) thick
slices
1 avocado pear, peeled,
stoned and sliced
1 box of mustard and cress
25 g (1 oz) sprouted alfalfa
or mung beans (p. 108)
50 g (2 oz) pecan nuts or
walnuts, shelled
65 ml (2½ fl oz) blue
cheese dressing (p. 99)
Small bunch of fresh
coriander leaves or flat-
leaved parsley, roughly
chopped

This crisp salad with its base of 'Iceberg' lettuce, colourful vegetables and blue cheese dressing makes a substantial main course dish. The ingredients can, of course, be varied according to season and taste. Here I have used a selection of crunchy vegetables with a garnish of fresh herbs. For a non-vegetarian salad, thin finger strips of meat or fish such as ham, tongue, salami, smoked mackerel, salmon eel or your favourite shellfish can be used.

Put the lettuce leaves in the bottom of a large salad bowl. Cook the beans in boiling water for 5 minutes, until just tender. Refresh under running water until cold. Add together with the broccoli, green pepper, celery, avocado, cress, bean sprouts and nuts.

Just before serving, add the blue cheese dressing to the salad and toss very carefully. Sprinkle with the coriander leaves or parsley and serve immediately.

FILLET OF BEEF NICOISE

S E R V E S
—— 8 ——

This is a delicious and elegant main course salad perfect for a summer lunch or a cold buffet. For the finest and most tender results, fillet of beef is used, but a less expensive cut of roasting beef, if well hung and perfectly cooked, is an excellent alternative. To save time, commercially prepared roast beef can also be used. The aubergine salad, although called niçoise after the tomatoes, olives and egg, is not the true salade niçoise from the south of France (p. 84), but one of the many variations. It can also be served as a salad on its own with crusty bread or as part of a selection of side salads.

Pre-heat the oven to gas mark 6, 400°F (200°C).

Tie the meat into a neat shape along its length. Brown evenly in the oil and butter. Set on a wire rack in a roasting dish and cook for 30–60 minutes, depending on the degree of 'rareness' required. Remove from the oven and cool. Wrap in aluminium foil and store in the refrigerator.

Aubergine slices can be sprinkled with salt and left to 'sweat' for 30 minutes before being washed and dried, a process known as *dégorger*. However, I find this an unnecessary preparation and fry the aubergine immediately after slicing. Fry them in batches in about 4 tablespoons of very hot oil in a large frying pan until brown on both sides. Drain well and put in a large bowl.

Fry the onion and garlic until soft but not coloured. Add the peppers and continue to fry until the onions begin to turn golden brown. Add the tomatoes, toss in the pan for a few minutes and put into the bowl with the aubergines.

While the vegetables are still warm, pour on the vinaigrette dressing and season with pepper. Toss lightly to coat with the dressing. Cover and chill until required.

When the meat is cold, carve thinly into about 28–30 slices and arrange in overlapping pieces in a semicircle on a large oval plate. Pile the aubergine salad in the space in front of the meat, and arrange the eggs with the olives on the salad. Garnish with watercress and serve immediately.

INGREDIENTS

FOR THE BEEF
1–1.25 kg (2–2½ lb) fillet of beef
1 tablespoon olive or sunflower oil
25 g (1 oz) butter
Freshly ground black pepper

FOR THE AUBERGINE SALAD
2 large aubergines, cut into 5 mm (¼ inch) slices
300 ml (10 fl oz) sunflower or olive oil
1 large onion, peeled and sliced
2 cloves garlic, peeled and crushed
2 large green peppers, de-seeded and cut into 3 mm × 5 cm (⅛ × 2 inch) strips
450 g (1 lb) tomatoes
3 tablespoons vinaigrette dressing (p. 95)
Freshly ground black pepper
4 hard-boiled eggs, quartered
50 g (2 oz) stoned black olives
1 bunch of watercress

BEEF TAPENADE

SERVES

— 4 —

*450 g (1 lb) roast beef, cut
into 1 cm (½ inch) slices*
*1 large green and 1 large
red pepper, de-seeded
and cut into 5 mm ×
5 cm (¼ × 2 inch) strips*
*4 tablespoons tapenade
purée (p. 97)*
*4 tablespoons vinaigrette
dressing (p. 95)*
12 stoned black olives
1 teaspoon capers, drained
*1 bunch of watercress, to
garnish*

Finger strips of tender cooked roast beef are dressed in
tapenade (p. 97) and served as a main meat dish with
watercress and mixed salad leaves.

Cut the roast beef into finger strips, approximately 6 cm
(2½ inch) long. Place the beef and the peppers in a large
mixing bowl.

Mix the tapenade and the French dressing together to
make a well blended sauce and pour over the beef and
peppers. Toss well to combine and coat. Cover and chill.

The beef always tastes better if left to marinate for a few
hours before serving, but if speed is required the salad can be
served immediately. Pile in a shallow serving dish, sprinkle
with the olives and capers and garnish with watercress.

SALT BEEF SALAD

S E R V E S

—— 4 ——

This is a spicy salad of salt beef and pickled gherkins served on a bed of potato mayonnaise and garnished with lettuce leaves and boiled beetroot. It looks stunning and tastes delicious. It is particularly quick and easy if commercially prepared potato salad and pre-cooked roast beef and beetroot are used. Only 10 minutes will be needed for boiling the eggs and combining the ingredients. Un-salted roast beef can also be used.

———

Combine the mustard, sugar and vinegar in a large bowl. Stir to blend. Add the beef and dill pickles to the dressing and toss gently. Cover and refrigerate while preparing the rest of the salad.

Cook the potatoes in their jackets until just tender. Peel and cut into 2.5 cm (1 inch) cubes. Place in a bowl and coat with the mayonnaise while still hot. Season with pepper.

Arrange the lettuce leaves around the edge of a large flat serving dish. Put the potato mayonnaise in the centre and flatten the surface. Pile the mustard beef on top of the potatoes. Place the eggs on the lettuce leaves around the edge of the plate, and arrange small piles of the beetroot between the eggs. Serve immediately.

INGREDIENTS

2 tablespoons mustard powder
1–1½ tablespoons muscovado sugar
2 tablespoons tarragon or wine vinegar
350 g (12 oz) salted brisket of beef, cut into 1 × 6 cm (½ × 2½ inch) slices
2 large pickled dill cucumbers, halved and cut into thin strips
4–6 large potatoes
65 ml (2½ fl oz) mayonnaise (p. 100)
Freshly ground black pepper
Lettuce leaves to serve
2 hard-boiled eggs, quartered
1 cooked beetroot, diced

*B*EAN &
SALAMI SALAD

S E R V E S
—— 4 ——

FOR THE SALAD

175 g (6 oz) French beans, fresh or frozen

175 g (6 oz) broad beans (shelled weight), fresh or frozen

6 tablespoons garlic and mustard dressing (p. 95)

100 g (4 oz) salami, finely shredded

8 spring onions, white and green, finely chopped

1 tablespoon mixed fresh herbs (parsley, oregano, tarragon), finely chopped

FOR THE SPICY MUSTARD DRESSING

To make about 150 ml (5 fl oz)

1 clove garlic, peeled and crushed

3 teaspoons mustard powder

¼ teaspoon muscovado sugar

¼ teaspoon salt

¼ teaspoon freshly ground black pepper

2 tablespoons red wine vinegar

4 drops of tabasco sauce

120 ml (4 fl oz) olive or sunflower oil

This is a filling main course salad, tossed while still hot in a spicy mustard dressing. The salami can be shredded more easily using kitchen scissors. Smoked ham makes an interesting alternative to the salami, and a small can of red kidney beans could be added to ring the changes.

Cook fresh beans together with a little boiling water to cover, for 3–5 minutes until just tender. Frozen beans will cook in about 3 minutes.

Drain and toss in the dressing while still hot. Transfer to a salad bowl and leave to cool. Stir in the remaining ingredients, tossing lightly to coat. Serve with a salad of mixed leaves.

For the dressing, combine the garlic, mustard powder, sugar, salt and pepper, vinegar and tabasco sauce in a screw-top jar and shake well to blend. Gradually add some of the oil to make a smooth paste; add the remaining oil to complete the dressing.

TRADITIONAL CORONATION CHICKEN SALAD

S E R V E S
— 4 —

There are many versions of this famous chicken salad created in honour of the Coronation of Queen Elizabeth II by the Cordon Bleu School of Cookery in London. The original version uses a subtle curry essence to flavour a rich mayonnaise. The 'cheat's' variety, although most acceptable, will only ever be a shadow of the real thing. However, for real speed, use commercial mayonnaise, curry paste and cooked chicken breast. If pre-cooked chicken breast meat is unavailable, raw chicken breast fillets cut into finger-sized slices can easily be cooked in boiling chicken stock while the coronation sauce is made. The curry essence is sufficient to flavour 600–900 ml (1–1½ pints) mayonnaise. For this recipe only 1½ teaspoons is required to produce a very mildly flavoured curried mayonnaise. The remaining essence freezes well.

━━━━━━

Prepare the curry essence by frying the onion in the oil until soft but not coloured. Stir in the curry paste or powder and fry for a few minutes to develop the flavours. Blend in the tomato purée, apricot jam, red wine, water, bay leaf and slices of lemon. Bring to the boil then reduce the heat and simmer for 10–15 minutes. Strain and cool.

Prepare the sauce by adding 1½ teaspoons of this curry essence to the mayonnaise, stirring well to blend.

Add the chicken to the coronation sauce and toss well to coat. Pile on to a shallow serving dish, dust with the paprika pepper and garnish with watercress. Serve with a Green rice salad (p. 44).

INGREDIENTS

FOR THE CURRY ESSENCE
2 tablespoons onion, peeled and finely chopped
1 tablespoon olive or sunflower oil
1 tablespoon mild curry powder or paste
1 teaspoon tomato purée
1 tablespoon smooth apricot jam
120 ml (4 fl oz) red wine
50 ml (2 fl oz) water
1 bay leaf
2 slices of lemon

FOR THE CHICKEN
300 ml (10 fl oz) mayonnaise (p. 100)
450 g (1 lb) cooked chicken breast fillet, cut into finger-sized slices
A pinch of paprika pepper
Watercress to garnish

CHICKEN &
PINEAPPLE SALAD

S E R V E S

—— 4 ——

*450 g (1 lb) cooked chicken
  breast fillet, cut into
  finger-sized slices*
*1 large sweet ripe
  pineapple*
*50 g (2 oz) walnuts,
  halved*
*150 ml (5 fl oz)
  mayonnaise*
*150 ml (5 fl oz) natural
  thick set yoghurt*
*Freshly ground black
  pepper*
¼ teaspoon paprika pepper
*Lettuce leaves and
  watercress to garnish*

This is a very quick and easy salad and particularly delicious when made with the flavoursome miniature pineapples that are sometimes available. It looks very attractive when served in the half pineapple shells, the miniature shells being used for individual portions, the larger pineapple shells forming part of a decorative display on the buffet table.

Place the chicken in a large mixing bowl. Cut the pineapple in half lengthwise through the shell, leaving the green top on for decoration. Using a grapefruit knife, cut round the outside edge of the pineapple between the flesh and skin to remove the flesh. Cut the flesh into oblong pieces, removing the core. Reserving a few pieces for garnish, add the pineapple pieces to the chicken. Add the walnut halves, reserving a few for the garnish. Toss to combine.

Mix the mayonnaise and yoghurt together and pour over the chicken, tossing the ingredients lightly. Season with ground pepper and if possible leave for 30 minutes to develop the flavours. Pile the chicken mixture into the pineapple shells, garnish with the paprika pepper and reserved pineapple pieces. Serve chilled on a bed of lettuce leaves garnished with watercress.

CHICKEN &
BEEF SATAY SALAD

S E R V E S

—— 4 ——

In traditional Malaysian satay, tender pieces of meat or vegetables are soaked in a spicy peanut marinade before being skewered, grilled and served with an equally hot and spicy sauce. In this cold satay salad, cooked chicken and beef are combined and coated in a satay dressing and served with a chunky cucumber salad. The salad can also be made entirely from beef or chicken.

———————

Prepare the satay dressing by frying the onion in the hot oil until soft but not coloured. Stir in the ground peanuts and chilli powder and fry for a few minutes to develop the flavour. Add the soy sauce, muscovado sugar, coconut, lemon rind and juice, stirring to combine. Bring to the boil, then reduce the heat and simmer for about 10 minutes; the liquid should be well reduced. Leave to cool, then stir in the natural yoghurt.

Add the beef and chicken to the satay dressing and toss well to coat. Arrange the salad leaves around the edge of the shallow serving dish and pile the beef and chicken in the centre. Dust with the paprika pepper and decorate with salted peanuts and coriander or parsley leaves. Serve with crunchy cucumber salad (p. 57).

INGREDIENTS

FOR THE SATAY DRESSING

1 small onion, peeled and grated

2 tablespoons olive or sunflower oil

50 g (2 oz) ground dry roasted peanuts

1/4–1/2 teaspoon chilli powder

1 tablespoon soy sauce

1 tablespoon muscovado sugar

100 g (4 oz) or 120 ml (4 fl oz) creamed coconut

Grated rind and juice of 1/2 lemon

150 ml (5 fl oz) natural thick set yoghurt

FOR THE SALAD

225 g (8 oz) cooked beef, cut into finger-sized slices

225 g (8 oz) cooked chicken, cut into finger-sized slices

Salad leaves for decoration

1/2 teaspoon paprika pepper

25 g (1 oz) salted peanuts

Fresh coriander leaves or broad-leaved parsley to garnish

SALADE NICOISE

S E R V E S

— 8 —

INGREDIENTS

2 large cooked potatoes,
   peeled, halved and cut
   into 1 cm (½ inch) slices
1 tablespoon onion, peeled
   and finely chopped
5–7 tablespoons vinaigrette
   dressing (p. 95)
100 g (4 oz) French beans,
   cut in half
Salt and freshly ground
   black pepper
1 head of crisp, firm lettuce
50 g (2 oz) cucumber, cut
   into 1 cm (½ inch) cubes
3 medium sized tomatoes,
   quartered
2 hard-boiled eggs,
   quartered
1 × 50 g (1¾ oz) tin of
   anchovy fillets, drained
1 × 200 g (7 oz) tin of
   tuna fish, drained
25–50 g (1–2 oz) black
   olives
1 tablespoon capers
1 tablespoon fresh parsley,
   finely chopped

Salade niçoise, as its name implies, comes from Nice in the south of France. It is one of the most famous salads from Provence and one of the best known of the 'composed' or mixed vegetable salads. There are, however, as with most classic dishes, many recipe variations and much debate about what a true niçoise salad should contain, even how it should be tossed and assembled. Although the ingredients will vary depending on the season and availability, they generally include hard-boiled eggs, tomatoes, green beans, potatoes, anchovies, tuna and olives with crisp lettuce leaves dressed in a light vinaigrette dressing, with or without garlic. My version, I hope, will satisfy all tastes and is certainly not complicated to make. In France, Salade niçoise is generally served as a first course, but it also makes a very colourful and nourishing main course dish for any time of year accompanied by crisp French bread, dry white wine, a little cheese and fruit to finish. These ingredients here will serve 4 as a main course. It is the perfect 'meal in minutes'.

Place the potato slices in a bowl with the onion and toss in 2 tablespoons of the vinaigrette dressing. Leave to cool.

Cook the beans in boiling salted water for about 5 minutes until just tender. Drain immediately and refresh under cold running water until completely cold. Dry well, turn into a bowl, season with salt and freshly ground black pepper and toss in 1 tablespoon of vinaigrette dressing.

Assemble the salad just before serving by separating the salad leaves and then tossing them in 2 tablespoons of the vinaigrette dressing. Lay these around the edge of a large round plate. Put the potatoes in the middle of the salad and arrange the green beans in a circle around them.

Arrange the cucumbers and tomatoes around the beans, dribbling a little vinaigrette dressing over them. Arrange the pieces of egg throughout the salad and drape the anchovies over them. Break the tuna fish into large flakes and pile in the centre of the potatoes. Dribble a tablespoon of vinaigrette over the top. Scatter the olives, capers and parsley over the salad and serve immediately.

HERRINGS IN SOURED CREAM

S E R V E S

— 4 —

Although this recipe uses home-marinated herrings, commercially prepared herrings can also be used. This makes the dish very quick and convenient as all that is required is for them to be drained, dried, mixed with the dressing and served.

Wash, gut and bone the herrings. Cut into fillets and then into 2.5 cm (1 inch) pieces. Put these into a deep glass or china bowl. Prepare the marinade by combining all the ingredients in a pan and bring to the boil. Simmer for about 1 minute. Remove from the heat and allow to cool. Pour over the herrings, cover and leave to marinate in the refrigerator for at least 6 hours. Remove the herring pieces from the marinade and dry on absorbent kitchen paper.

Combine the soured cream, red onion and spring onion in a large bowl. Stir in the marinated herring pieces and season with pepper.

Arrange the prepared salad leaves on four individual plates. Place the potato in overlapping slices in the centre of the salad leaves. Divide the herrings in their sour cream dressing between the four plates piling them on top of the potatoes. Sprinkle with the chives.

INGREDIENTS

FOR THE SALAD
4 large herrings
Mixed salad leaves
8 small cooked potatoes,
  sliced thinly

FOR THE MARINADE
150 ml (5 fl oz) cider
  vinegar
150 ml (5 fl oz) water
3 tablespoons caster sugar
1 small onion, peeled and
  sliced
1–2 bay leaves
6 peppercorns
6 allspice berries
A few stalks of fennel,
  (optional)

**FOR THE SOUR CREAM
DRESSING**
300 ml (10 fl oz) soured
  cream
1 small red onion, peeled,
  quartered and sliced
4 tablespoons spring onion,
  chopped
Freshly ground black
  pepper
1 tablespoon chives, finely
  chopped

SMOKED
MUSSEL & RICE SALAD

SERVES
—— 4 ——

INGREDIENTS

100 g (4 oz) cooked long-grain rice
2 × 105 g (4 oz) cans of smoked mussels, drained
1 small onion, peeled and finely chopped
4 celery stalks
100 g (4 oz) mushrooms, sliced
3 tablespoons vinaigrette dressing (see p. 95)
3 tablespoons mussel oil
Salt and freshly ground black pepper
2 tablespoons parsley, finely chopped
Mixed salad leaves to serve

Canned smoked mussels are one of the most tasty and convenient fish products available and certainly a valuable asset for any quick salad cook. Although not the cheapest of products, their distinctive flavour combines well with other ingredients, making a little go a long way. Smoked oysters can also be used for this recipe.

Place the cold rice in a large mixing bowl.

Reserve the oil from the mussels. Add the mussels to the rice along with the onion.

Cut the celery into 2.5 cm (1 inch) lengths and then into thin strips about 3 mm (1/8 inch) wide; add to the rice and mussels, together with the sliced mushrooms.

Combine the vinaigrette dressing and 3 tablespoons of the reserved fish oil in a screw-top jar, shaking well to combine.

Pour the dressing over the ingredients in the bowl and toss gently to combine and moisten. Season to taste with the salt, pepper and parsley. Arrange the prepared mixed salad leaves on four main course plates and divide the mussel and rice salad between them. Serve well chilled.

PORTABLE SALADS

Although salads are very versatile, traditional creations are difficult to transport, hard to keep fresh and not always convenient to eat, particularly if you are half-way up a mountain!

However, when conveniently packaged, easily carried salads can be made for work, travel, hiking trips or even a relaxing picnic. Plate, cutlery and containers are dispensed with and replaced by a much more convenient and edible package. This can be as simple as two slices of bread or as imaginative as a Lebanese pitta bread pocket. For today the salad sandwich has been revolutionised not only by more sophisticated and discerning palates and adventurous requirements but by the wide variety of tasty packaging now available. Crusty rolls, crisp French sticks, crunchy taco shells, soft baps and soda farls, bagels and pizza bases, pitta bread, rye bread, potato and milk bread are now available in almost every supermarket and delicatessen throughout the country. Even the traditional British loaf has once more become interesting with the return of a wide range of flours, a multitude of seeds, grains and flavourings, all of which provide a rich variety of taste and texture.

The packaging, however, is not the sole contribution to perfection of this portable product. Salad fillings have become more sophisticated and the imagination is totally free to invent such combinations as blue cheese, celery and date; avocado and chrysanthemum leaves; and smoked ham, anchovies and olives. The possibilities are endless. Here are a few of my more subdued ideas – the more outrageous, I will leave to *your* imagination!

FRENCH FLUTES

Crusty French sticks (baguettes), or flutes as they are sometimes called, make excellent protective packages for tender salad leaves and other delicate ingredients, as well as offering a tasty filling alternative to the softer type rolls and breads. They transport well either whole or in more manageable sized portions. The most famous of these is the French *Pan Bagnia*, which literally means 'wet bread'. These French 'sandwiches' are sold in all the cafés along the coast of Provence and on into the Italian Riviera. Although French bread is the most frequently used and widely available, in France other small round country breads are also used, and in the Nice area a special loaf is even baked for the purpose. All types of fillings are acceptable along with the tradition of moistening the bread with olive oil before filling.

Pan Bagnia Slice a French stick along the side through its length. Sprinkle the inside with a little olive oil or butter if preferred. Arrange lettuce leaves, torn into reasonable size pieces, over the bottom half of the bread and arrange sliced tomatoes, hard-boiled egg, anchovies and olives on top. Season with freshly ground black pepper and cover with the top half of the bread. Tie at intervals with string or cut into four. Wrap in greaseproof paper to transport.

Niçoise filling Here the traditional niçoise mixture of hard-boiled eggs, tomatoes, green beans, anchovies, tuna fish and olives is arranged on top of a bed of shredded lettuce leaves on the bottom half of the French flute, the top half acting as the lid to sandwich the filling together. (See Salad niçoise p. 84).

Lettuce, blue cheese and dates Pieces of crisp lettuce leaves are arranged on the bottom half of the French flute and covered with pieces of blue cheese, sliced stoned dates and thin slices of crisp green apple, before being encased by the top half of the French flute.

Ham, cheese, chutney and stuffed olives I generally like to use a lightly smoked ham for this filling along with thin slices of Swiss cheese such as Emmental or Gruyère and some home-made chutney. Line the bottom half of the French flute with the ham and top with the cheese. Spread the chutney sparingly over the cheese, add the sliced stuffed olives before covering with the top half of the bread.

Mozzarella, tomato and avocado Line the bottom half of the French flute with torn salad leaves and arrange alternate slices of Mozzarella cheese, tomatoes and avocado pear (sprinkled with a little lemon juice to keep its colour) on top. Season with freshly ground black pepper and a sprinkling of fresh basil leaves if available. Cover with the top of the French flute.

PITTA POCKETS

White or wholemeal Lebanese bread makes a wonderful package for any type of salad ingredients, because it can so easily be made into a pouch. To do this, grill the flatter side lightly under a pre-heated grill; this will make the bread puff up and enable it to be opened for filling. Once toasted, cut the pitta bread in half across the middle and stuff with one of the following fillings:

Lettuce, spinach, bean sprouts and cottage cheese Line the pitta halves with shredded lettuce and spinach leaves. Mix some cottage cheese with a few chopped walnuts and pile on top of the green leaves. Sprinkle a generous handful of well washed and dried bean sprouts on top of the cottage cheese.

Feta cheese, olives, tomatoes and lettuce Line the pitta halves with crisp shredded lettuce leaves. Add a thick layer of well flavoured sliced tomatoes and season with freshly ground black pepper. Scatter a few torn, fresh basil leaves on top; add pieces of feta cheese and top with stoned black or green olives.

Taramasalata and tuna salad Line the pitta halves with crisp shredded salad leaves. Mix a small can of drained tuna fish with about 1 tablespoon of taramasalata (p. 106). Season with freshly ground black pepper and a dash of lemon juice. Pile into the pitta halves and top with diced cucumber and alfalfa sprouts (see p. 108).

Chicken and grape salad Line the pitta halves with crisp shredded lettuce. Combine pieces of cooked diced chicken, halved seedless grapes and chopped celery with enough curried mayonnaise (see p. 101) to blend. Season with freshly ground black pepper and pile the salad on top of the shredded lettuce.

TACO SHELLS

Mexican taco shells – thin flat cakes made from stoneground wheat or maize flour, fried and shaped – make wonderful packages for all types of salad fillings, for a quick and easy snack or meal. These dry shells which have a long shelf life are sold in boxes and are readily available. Before using they should be warmed in the oven at gas mark 4, 350°F (180°C) for 10 minutes. The shells will crisp on cooling and when cold are ready to be filled. Because they are quite brittle, they need to be packed in a rigid container for transportation.

Mexican salad Line the prepared taco shells with shredded lettuce or cabbage leaves. Prepare a filling of cooked red kidney beans, finely diced red pepper and chopped fried bacon. Mix with grated cheddar cheese and a little sour cream, then pile into the taco shells.

Chicken guacamole Line the prepared taco shells with shredded lettuce or salad leaves. Mash the flesh of a large avocado pear with a little lemon juice and a few drops of tabasco sauce. Add a large tomato, roughly chopped, with a small piece of chopped onion and some chopped, fresh coriander. Stir in some shredded pieces of cooked chicken and pile into the taco shells. Garnish with fresh coriander leaves.

SALAD ADDITIONS

The extras, or additions, that are added to a salad are just as important as the salad itself, because without them the salad, whether simple or elaborate, would be reduced to its original standing of a dull and boring, sad and jaded dish, totally lacking sparkle and inspiration.

Additions do not have to be expensive or complicated: a sprinkling of parsley or finely snipped chives over a potato mayonnaise; an oil and vinegar dressing of the finest quality in which to toss a small selection of salad leaves and herbs; or crunchy garlic flavoured croûtons.

Apart from dressings and garnishes, there are many other interesting items which can turn an everyday salad into a special occasion dish – additions such as nuts, plain or roasted, chopped or whole; seeds such as sesame, fennel and caraway, added just as they are or roasted to develop their flavour; and sprouted seeds, grains and beans, which not only are highly nutritious but also have a most interesting appearance, taste and texture.

There are also numerous dips without which a plate of raw salad ingredients would certainly be incomplete, dips such as avocado, tofu, hummus (the popular Middle Eastern dip made from chickpeas), and tahini, a sesame seed paste.

In the next few pages I consider some of these additions in detail and I explain how to develop a kitchen garden of beans and seeds, on the windowsill.

OILS

Oil is one of the most essential elements of a good salad being the major constituent of both vinaigrette dressing and mayonnaise. The word 'oil' comes from the Latin *olea*, and indeed *olive oil* has long been regarded as the finest oil for all culinary purposes, particularly that of salad dressings. Good quality olive oil has a soft rich and full bodied aroma and flavour. The best oils are extracted from ripe or partially ripe olives from Italy, France, Spain and Greece. All quality oils are extracted from the olives under pressure, without the addition of chemicals or water. The 'first pressing' after separating and filtering is the finest quality, most expensive olive oil and on labels this is referred to as 'first cold pressed', or 'extra virgin oil'. Second pressed oils have cold water added to the remaining pulp and are labelled 'fine' or 'extra fine', or sometimes 'virgin oil'. They have a slightly sharper flavour and are consequently less expensive. A further pressing, using hot water, is done to produce a third grade olive oil referred to as 'pure' olive oil. This has too strong and coarse a flavour for a salad dressing.

The use of olive oil in salad dressings has an added advantage in that it is thought that it may help reduce the level of cholesterol in the blood – thus contributing an important health benefit. However, because of its distinctive and strongly fruity flavour, olive oil dressings are very much an acquired taste. Some supermarkets are now producing their own label 'extra virgin cold pressed' olive oil which is not only an excellent quality but also a reasonable price.

Sunflower oil is another oil which is even more versatile but rather tasteless. This oil is pale in colour and very neutral in flavour and lends itself well to the addition of other flavourings such as herbs and spices.

Between these two extremes of flavour is a wide spectrum of other oils. Less distinctive oils include *safflower oil* which is light in colour and high in polyunsaturates; *peanut oil* which is inclined to have a heavy oil texture and poor flavour; *corn oil*, bland but useful when very little flavour is required in the dressing; *rapeseed oil*, light and pale in colour with a rich nutty flavour; *almond oil*, a delicate nut oil with a rich flavour but not easy to find even in specialist shops; *hazelnut oil*, more readily available and with a deep nutty flavour combining well with tart green leaves; and *French walnut oil*, one of the most luxurious oils.

Soya bean oil has a strong flavour and if used for salad dressing should be well diluted with a bland oil like saf-flower or sunflower. *Chinese sesame oil*, made from toasted sesame seeds, should also be diluted in the same way as its taste is so distinctive and overpowering it can completely block out all other flavours. The *light sesame oil* in contrast, pressed from raw white seeds, is pale yellow in colour and delicately mild and pleasant to the taste.

Most oils, particularly olive oil, benefit from being sealed well after use and stored away from direct sunlight. Nut oils should only be bought in small quantities because they become rancid in a few months. They should be kept in the refrigerator. Olive oil, in contrast, is not improved by being refrigerated; indeed it only requires a cool dark place and will keep for up to a year, if given the chance!

Herb-flavoured oils can easily be made by combining ¼ cup of chopped herbs with 2 cups of a neutral flavoured oil in a jar, sealing well and leaving to infuse for about 10 days, shaking occasionally. The oil is then strained through muslin into a screw-top bottle (an empty oil bottle is ideal), labelled and stored in a dark cool place. Herb-flavoured oil will keep for 2–3 months.

VINEGARS

Salad dressings and mayonnaise must also include an acid, usually vinegar but sometimes lemon or lime juice. Vinegar is produced by the acid fermentation of an alcoholic liquid, most commonly red or white wine, but also cider, malt or rice. The result is vinegar, from the French *vin-aigre* – 'sour wine'.

As with oils there are also several types of vinegar, each with a different flavour, strength and quality which will add their own distinctive taste to the dressing. Some of the best vinegars are the wine vinegars from Orleans in the Loire region of France, the Balsamics from Modena in Italy, and the sherry vinegars from Spain. Athough many of these are only just beginning to become popular, they are fairly widely available. They are, however, inclined to be expensive. The advantage of using such high quality vinegars is that they are so concentrated that a little will go a long way.

There are two vinegars which are probably more common in kitchens than those already mentioned, *malt vinegar* and *distilled white vinegar*. Malt vinegar is made from grain and cider vinegar, and white vinegar from various grains. Both are very sharp and acidic and their taste rather too strong and unrefined for delicate salad dressing.

Red wine vinegar can be made from any red wine and has a sharp, sweet, full-bodied flavour. It combines well with olive and nut oils and makes a dressing which is very complementary to highly flavoured salad greens. *White wine vinegar* tends to be sweeter and combines well with the milder salad leaves.

Cider vinegar is made from apples, tastes of the fruit and has a strong bite. It should be used sparingly. It contains malic acid which aids the digestive process.

Sherry vinegar is a by-product of sherry and the best comes from Spain. It is aged in wooden barrels which gives a rich, full, smooth flavour with a slight sharpness. It combines beautifully with olive and nut oils.

Balsamic vinegar is a rich reddish-brown vinegar from Italy produced from a sweet wine and aged for varying lengths of time in wooden barrels which gives it a smooth rich flavour. These, along with the sherry vinegars of Spain, are my favourite vinegars for French dressings.

Flavoured vinegars include those flavoured with ingredients such as chillies, garlic, peppercorns, herbs, fruit, flowers and petals, and have become increasingly popular in recent years. Although they are expensive to buy, they are inexpensive and easy to make.

Herb-infused vinegar Use 25 g (1 oz) of fresh herbs such as rosemary, sage, oregano, bay leaves and thyme, or a combination, to every 600 ml (1 pint) white wine vinegar. Put the wine vinegar in an earthenware or glass crock. Add the herbs, stirring to infuse, and leave for 2–4 weeks, stirring occasionally. Strain through muslin into sterilised glass bottles and add a stalk of the fresh herb as a 'label'. Seal with a cork stopper.

Fruit vinegar Use 50 g (2 oz) lightly bruised soft fruits such as strawberries, raspberries, blueberries, blackberries, pears, peaches or plums to every 600 ml (1 pint) white wine vinegar. Put the wine vinegar and fruit into an earthenware or glass crock. Cover and leave to infuse for 2 days. Pour into a saucepan, bring to boiling point, strain through cheesecloth and pour into sterilised bottles. Cork and label.

In the following recipes for salad dressings, the best oils to use are either extra virgin olive oil, or sunflower oil if a more neutral oil is required. Where different types, combinations or flavoured oils are required, they are generally specified. However, cooking is all about experimenting so do try other combinations.

*V*INAIGRETTE OR FRENCH DRESSING

This is the most widely used salad dressing and forms the basis of many other dressings. Its correct name is 'vinaigrette' although it is often more commonly referred to as 'French dressing'. It is a combination of oil and vinegar, with the proportions varying depending on the result required and indeed the person making the dressing. The Romans have a saying that it takes four people to make a salad – a miser to put in the vinegar, a spendthrift to add the oil, a wise man to season it and a madman to toss it.

There are a variety of ways of making vinaigrette dressing. The salt and pepper can be put into a salad or small bowl along with the vinegar and stirred with a wooden spoon or whisked until the salt has dissolved. The oil is then added very gradually until the mixture thickens slightly. Alternatively all the ingredients can be combined in a screw-top jar and shaken vigorously until an emulsion is formed. When making large quantities of vinaigrette dressing, the ingredients can be combined in a food processor. However, care has to be taken making vinaigrette this way as it can very easily become too thick like mayonnaise.

Garlic vinaigrette Pound one clove of peeled garlic to a purée in the salad bowl before adding the vinegar and oil; or crush the garlic before combining with the other ingredients in a screw-top jar or food processor.

Mustard vinaigrette Mix 1–2 tablespoons of Dijon mustard with the salt and pepper before adding the vinegar and oil or combining with the other ingredients as above.

Herb vinaigrette Any vinaigrette can be combined with chopped fresh herbs such as parsley, basil, mint or marjoram. Add these after the vinaigrette has been mixed.

INGREDIENTS

To make about 300 ml (10 fl oz)
250 ml (8 fl oz) olive or sunflower oil
4 tablespoons wine vinegar
1–2 teaspoons salt
½ teaspoon freshly ground black pepper

CITRUS DRESSING

To make about 250 ml (8 fl oz)

200 ml (7 fl oz) olive, sunflower, sesame or nut oil

Grated rind of ½ lemon or orange

Juice of ½ lemon, orange or grapefruit

A pinch of sugar

½ teaspoon salt

Freshly ground black pepper (optional)

This is a variation on the basic vinaigrette dressing and is excellent for fruit-based salads or light combinations where fruit is used. The oil can be olive, sunflower, sesame or nut oil, and the citrus juice, which replaces the vinegar, either orange, lemon or grapefruit, depending on the salad ingredients to be dressed and, of course, individual taste. The lightness of the dressing can also be altered by the proportion of oil to juice.

Combine all the ingredients in a screw-top jar and shake vigorously to form an emulsion. Adjust the seasoning and store in the refrigerator. Use as required.

WALNUT DRESSING

To make this dressing, use the same ingredients, measures and method as for the Vinaigrette/French Dressing on page 95, but instead substitute walnut oil for olive or sunflower oil.

Dressings using nut oils need to be stored in the refrigerator.

TAPENADE

This is a deliciously rich purée of capers, olives and anchovies, from Provence. It takes its name from the old Provençal word *tapena*, meaning caper, one of its main ingredients. It can be used in a great variety of ways and for many different purposes, from a simple first course, a quick snack or a light lunch, to a picnic. It can be served as a dip for crudités (see p. 31) and hard-boiled eggs; as a pâté to spread on toast or crisp french bread; as a stuffing for hard-boiled eggs, the yolks being mixed with the tapenade paste and then returned to the shells; or combined with vinaigrette and used as a dressing for salads and cold meats. This rich dark paste with its powerful piquant flavour will also keep well for several weeks in a sealed jar in the refrigerator.

Place the olives, anchovy fillets, capers, tuna fish, lemon juice and mustard in a food processor and blend until a very smooth paste has formed. Then, still blending, very gradually add the oil just as though you were making mayonnaise, until the mixture resembles a thick paste. Taste and season with a little more lemon juice if necessary. Add the brandy if being used. Spoon into a glass or earthenware jar, cover and store in the refrigerator until required.

INGREDIENTS

To make about 250 ml (8 fl oz)

150 g (5 oz) stoned black olives

1 × 50 g (1¾ oz) tin of anchovy fillets, drained and rinsed

3 tablespoons capers, drained

50 g (2 oz) tuna fish, drained

Juice of 1 small lemon

½ teaspoon Dijon mustard

65 ml (2½ fl oz) olive or sunflower oil

1 tablespoon brandy (optional)

PIQUANT DRESSING

This is a spicy variation on the basic vinaigrette and will keep for several weeks in a refrigerator.

INGREDIENTS

To make about 300 ml (10 fl oz)
200 ml (7 fl oz) olive or sunflower oil
65 ml (2½ fl oz) wine or cider vinegar
2 cloves garlic, peeled and crushed
2 teaspoons muscovado sugar
½ teaspoon tabasco sauce
2 teaspoons soya sauce
¼ teaspoon salt
½ teaspoon Dijon mustard
Freshly ground black pepper

Combine all the ingredients in a screw-top jar and shake vigorously to form an emulsion. Store in the refrigerator and use as required.

ORIENTAL DRESSING

This spicy dressing, both piquant and hot, makes a most interesting dressing.

INGREDIENTS

To make about 200 ml (7 fl oz)
120 ml (4 fl oz) olive or sunflower oil
25 ml (1 fl oz) light sesame seed oil
3 tablespoons red wine vinegar
2 cloves garlic, peeled and crushed
3 tablespoons soy sauce
½ teaspoon tabasco sauce
½ teaspoon black pepper
¼ teaspoon muscovado sugar

Combine all the ingredients in a screw-top jar and shake vigorously to form an emulsion. Store covered in the refrigerator, but allow to return to room temperature before using.

SILKEN TOFU DRESSING

This is a smooth light and nutritious salad dressing made from soya bean curd and natural yoghurt. Serve with crudités or as a dressing for other salad ingredients.

Combine all the ingredients in a food processor and blend until smooth.

Tarragon tofu dressing Tarragon tofu dressing is an excellent accompaniment for dessert or avocado pears. Other herbs such as marjoram and fennel can be used and lemon juice can replace the vinegar. To make about 300 ml (10 fl oz), which will coat four to six pears, combine the tofu with 3–4 tablespoons tarragon or pear vinegar, 2–3 tablespoons finely chopped fresh tarragon and freshly ground black pepper.

INGREDIENTS

To make about 450 ml (15 fl oz)
1 × 297 g (10½ oz) carton firm silken tofu
150 ml (5 fl oz) natural yoghurt
Juice of 1 lemon
2 tablespoons white wine or tarragon vinegar

BLUE CHEESE DRESSING

This is a tangy salad dressing suitable for well-flavoured robust vegetables or leaves. A wide variety of blue cheeses are available but it is best to choose one of the harder varieties such as Stilton, Shropshire, blue Cheshire, or Danish blue.

Combine all the ingredients in a food processor and process until smooth. It may be necessary to add a little extra vinaigrette dressing, soured cream or yoghurt, to achieve a true consistency of thin cream.

INGREDIENTS

To make about 300 ml (10 fl oz)
75 g (3 oz) blue cheese, rinded and crumbled
1 tablespoon lemon juice
1 clove garlic, peeled and crushed
150 ml (5 fl oz) soured cream or natural yoghurt
3 tablespoons mayonnaise (p. 100)
3 tablespoons French dressing (p. 95)
Freshly ground black pepper
2 tablespoons parsley, finely chopped

99

MAYONNAISE

To make about 300 ml
(10 fl oz)
2 egg yolks
¼ teaspoon mustard
powder
300 ml (10 fl oz) olive or
sunflower oil
1–2 tablespoons lemon
juice or wine vinegar
A pinch of powdered white
pepper
¼ teaspoon salt

Home-made mayonnaise is a revelation to those who have never tasted it. This smooth emulsion of egg yolks, olive oil and lemon juice or wine vinegar is quick and easy to make, forms the basis of many other salad sauces, and is used to enhance all types of cooked and raw foods particularly salad ingredients. Mayonnaise based on fresh unpasteurised raw egg cannot be made commercially, but it can be made at home in small quantities for *immediate* consumption.

For small quantities, a hand-held electric whisk is the most satisfactory method. The result is thinner and much less sticky and aerated. To obtain the best results the eggs and oil should be at room temperature, the eggs beaten on their own for about 1–2 minutes until slightly thickened, and the oil added gradually at first to prevent curdling. If the mixture does curdle, try adding a tablespoon of boiling water and beating hard. If this fails to thicken it, start again with a fresh egg yolk, adding the curdled mixture drop by drop until it is absorbed. Mayonnaise should be kept in the refrigerator and only for a couple of days if well covered.

Put the yolks and mustard into a medium size bowl and beat for ½–1 minute with an electric whisk until pale and thick. Begin adding the oil, drop by drop, beating continually until about half the oil has been added. At this stage the oil can now be added in a very slow stream, still beating constantly. When the mixture is very thick, add the lemon juice or vinegar and then continue adding the rest of the oil. Season to taste, adding pepper and extra lemon juice or vinegar as required. If the mayonnaise is too thick, a little hot water can be added to bring it to the correct consistency. Transfer the mayonnaise to a smaller bowl or a jar, cover carefully to prevent a skin from forming on the surface, and then store in the refrigerator. Let the mayonnaise return to room temperature to prevent it becoming oily and try to use as soon as possible.

Mayonnaise made in the food processor This is a very quick and easy way to make mayonnaise, giving an excellent silky smooth result. Substitute a whole egg for one of the yolks and blend with the mustard. Add the oil in a thin stream while still blending. When the mixture thickens, scrape the sides of the bowl. Add the lemon juice or vinegar and season to taste when it is very thick.

Curried mayonnaise Gradually add 300 ml (10 fl oz) mayonnaise to ½–1 tablespoon of curry paste and use to coat vegetables such as cauliflower, coleslaw, cabbage, and boiled potatoes.

Garlic mayonnaise Pound 3 cloves of garlic in a mortar until a paste is formed. Alternatively the garlic can be crushed on a chopping board using the blade of a knife. Add the mixture to the yolks, mustard and pepper before beating in the oil.

Mustard mayonnaise Stir in 1–2 tablespoons coarse grain or Dijon mustard to 300 ml (10 fl oz) mayonnaise.

Herb mayonnaise Stir 1 teaspoon each of finely chopped tarragon, parsley, chervil and chives into the prepared mayonnaise.

Mango mayonnaise Purée the flesh of one ripe mango and add to the mayonnaise with 1 teaspoon finely chopped lemon mint or lemon balm.

Mayonnaise chantilly Not more than 2 hours before serving, fold 2 tablespoons lemon juice into 300 ml (10 fl oz) mayonnaise. Fold in 150 ml (5 fl oz) whipped cream along with salt and pepper to taste if necessary.

AVOCADO DIP

S E R V E S

—— 4 ——

2 ripe avocado pears
2 tablespoons lemon juice
2 drops tabasco sauce
½ tablespoon onion, peeled
  and grated
Salt and freshly ground
  black pepper
A pinch of chilli powder

This smooth purée made from the flesh of avocado pears, makes an excellent salad dip for crisp new vegetables as well as a topping for portable salads and sandwiches. Ripe unblemished avocado pears should be used and lemon juice added to prevent the dip from discolouring.

Halve the avocados lengthwise and remove the stones. Scoop out the flesh and put in a bowl along with the lemon juice, tabasco sauce, grated onion, salt and pepper and chilli powder. Mash with a fork until very smooth and the consistency of thick cream.

Pile into a serving bowl and serve immediately or cover and chill before serving. Avocado dip should be prepared no more than 3 hours in advance as it can easily lose its colour.

TOFU & STILTON DIP

S E R V E S

—— 4 ——

1 × 297 g (10½ oz) firm
  silken tofu
275 g (10 oz) Stilton
  cheese
1 clove garlic, peeled and
  crushed
1 tablespoon lemon juice
1 tablespoon finely snipped
  chives

Any type of blue cheese can be used in this recipe, depending on the strength of flavour required. Serve with crisp, strong-tasting salad leaves.

Combine the tofu, cheese, garlic and lemon juice in a food processor and blend to form a smooth thick consistency. Transfer to a serving bowl, stir in the chives and serve as a dip with crudités (p. 31), pitta bread, cheese biscuits or straws.

PITTA POCKETS WITH LETTUCE, SPINACH, BEAN SPROUTS AND COTTAGE CHEESE (PAGE 89); TACO SHELLS WITH MEXICAN SALAD (PAGE 90) AND FRENCH FLUTES WITH MOZZARELLA, TOMATO AND AVOCADO (PAGE 89)

HUMMUS

SERVES

—— 4 ——

This thick rich purée made from chick peas and tahini, a sesame seed paste, is sold in jars and is a speciality of the Middle East. It is served either as a pâté or a dip with pitta bread or crudités (p. 31). Hummus can be made from dried chick peas which require soaking overnight followed by several hours cooking, but for speed, use canned chick peas, which, although more expensive, are much more convenient.

———

Place the chick peas in a food processor with the garlic, lemon juice, tahini paste, pepper and salt. Blend until a very smooth paste has formed. Gradually add the oil until the mixture is rich and thick. Finally blend in the yoghurt.

Pile into one large or four small serving bowls. Sprinkle with paprika pepper and eat by scooping up with pieces of vegetables or warm pitta bread.

INGREDIENTS

1 × 400 g (14 oz) tin of chick peas, drained and rinsed
2 cloves garlic, peeled and crushed
2–3 tablespoons lemon juice
150 ml (5 fl oz) tahini paste
Freshly ground black pepper
1 teaspoon salt
150 ml (5 fl oz) olive or sunflower oil
6 tablespoons thick set natural yoghurt
1 teaspoon paprika pepper

TROPICAL FRUIT SALAD IN GINGER SYRUP (PAGE 118)

TARAMASALATA

SERVES

—— 4 ——

This Greek speciality made from smoked fish roe beaten with lemon juice, olive oil and bread into a light fluffy mixture, can be served either as a spread, pâté or a dip, depending on its consistency.

INGREDIENTS

2 slices of white bread, crusts removed
100 ml (3½ fl oz) cold water
225 g (8 oz) smoked cod's roe, skinned
1 clove garlic, peeled and crushed
2 tablespoons lemon juice
300 ml (10 fl oz) olive oil
Freshly ground black pepper
1 tablespoon parsley, finely chopped

Soak the bread in the water for about 5 minutes. Gently squeeze out the excess liquid and place in a processor with the cod's roe, garlic and lemon juice. Process until very smooth and well blended. Very gradually add the oil, processing constantly until it has all been incorporated.

Season with pepper and pile into one serving bowl or individual bowls. Sprinkle with parsley and serve with pitta bread, crackers or a selection of raw vegetables.

BAGNA CAUDA

(Hot anchovy and garlic dip)

SERVES

—— 4 ——

This rich creamy Italian dip is served hot with a selection of raw vegetables or bread sticks and is truly delicious.

INGREDIENTS

450 ml (15 fl oz) double cream
50 g (2 oz) unsalted butter
8 anchovy fillets, drained and finely chopped
3 cloves garlic, peeled and crushed

Bring the cream to the boil in a large heavy pan and cook, stirring frequently, for about 15–20 minutes, until it has thickened and reduced by about half.

Melt the butter in a flameproof casserole (choose one suitable to bring to the table) over a low heat without browning. Add the anchovies and the garlic, then stir in the reduced cream. Return to the boil stirring constantly and serve immediately with individual plates of raw vegetables. Eat by dipping the vegetables or bread sticks into the hot sauce.

MUSHROOM & HERB DIP

S E R V E S
—— 4 ——

This rich, well flavoured and substantial dip is excellent with fingers of hot toast, pitta bread or a selection of crudités (p. 31).

━━━━

Heat the oil in a large frying pan and fry the onion until soft but not coloured. Add the mushrooms and continue to cook over a gentle heat until soft and beginning to colour slightly. Add the ground coriander and fry for a further few minutes to develop the flavour. Cool before turning into a food processor.

Add the remainder of the ingredients and process until the mixture is smooth and fine. Scrape the purée well down from the sides of the bowl several times during the processing to make sure it is evenly blended. Chill before serving.

INGREDIENTS

To make about 350 ml
  or (12 fl oz)
*2 tablespoons olive or
  sunflower oil*
*1 small onion, peeled and
  finely chopped*
*225 g (8 oz) mushrooms,
  sliced*
*1 teaspoon ground
  coriander*
1 tablespoon fresh coriander
*100 g (4 oz) low fat cream
  cheese*
*65 ml (2½ fl oz) fromage
  frais*
*1 teaspoon Worcestershire
  sauce*
*Freshly ground black
  pepper*

SEEDS & SPROUTS

One of the most valuable additions to any salad is the sprouted bean – very inexpensive and a storehouse of nutritional goodness. Bean sprouts are ready to harvest when they are between 5 mm–4 cm (¼–1½ inch) long, that is after only 3–4 days.

One of the best known of the sprouts is the Chinese mung bean, but there are many other seeds, grains and beans such as adzuki, lima, alfalfa and wheat that can easily be sprouted on your own windowsill. No soil, garden or special equipment is required for growing sprouts, just natural light and somewhere warm to germinate the seeds.

There are many ways of sprouting seeds – in glass jars, bowls, dishes, plastic boxes, seed trays, or in one of the many patented sprouters now on the market. To find which is the best for you is really a matter of experimenting. When I need large quantities of sprouts, particularly for my commercial kitchen, I use a seed tray with drainage holes, and lined with nylon mesh, which enables the seeds to drain better.

The main principles to be remembered when sprouting seeds are: a) grow them no deeper than 1 cm (½ inch) deep; b) soak them overnight before sowing; c) rinse them in cold water morning and evening; d) ensure that they have good drainage otherwise they will rot; e) grow them in a warm place at 55–70°F (13–24°C), either in the dark or in the light, depending on whether crisp light-coloured sprouts or soft green sprouts are required; and f) harvest them when young and tender. The seeds will be ready to harvest in 3 to 4 days. Rinse and drain well before putting into a polythene bag and storing. Sometimes I even put the entire seed tray in the fridge once the sprouts have reached their optimum size which helps extend their life. The sprouts are delicious either on their own, in a salad entirely made up of different types of sprouted seeds or added to salad leaves and other salad ingredients.

N.B. There are many different seeds suitable for sprouting but not all can be used raw: indeed some such as red kidney beans, tomato seeds and seed potatoes should not be sprouted at all because they are poisonous. The seeds I have suggested in the following chart can all be sprouted and used raw.

SUITABLE SEEDS FOR SPROUTING

SEED/GRAIN	AVERAGE TIME IN DAYS	LENGTH OF SPROUT
SMALL SEEDS		
Alfalfa	3–4	2.5–5 cm (1–2 in)
Fenugreek	3–4	1 cm (½ in)
Radish	3–5	1–2.5 cm (½–1 in)
LARGER SEEDS		
Lentil	3–5	5 mm–2.5 cm (¼–1 in)
Adzuki beans	3–5	1–2.5 cm (½–1 in)
Mung	2–6	1–6 cm (½–2½ in)
Lima	3–5	1–4 cm (½–1½ in)
Chick peas – soak for 18 hours changing water twice	4–5	1 cm (½ in)
GRAINS		
Wheat	4–5	1–1.5 cm (½–¾ in)
Rye	3–5	2.5–5 cm (1–2 in)
Barley	3–5	1 cm (½ in)

GARLIC CROUTONS

INGREDIENTS

To make about 75 g
  (3oz)
*3 slices white or wholemeal
  bread, approximately
  100 g (4 oz), 5 mm
  (¼ inch) thick*
*2 cloves garlic, peeled and
  crushed*
4–5 tablespoons olive oil

These highly flavoured, crispy cubes of bread are a very useful addition in the salad kitchen and are quickly and easily prepared. They also keep well if stored in an airtight container and are then always to hand for garnishing a soup or a salad.

Remove the crusts from the bread and cut into 5 mm (¼ inch) cubes. Pound the garlic to a smooth paste with the end of a rolling pin or a pestle. Gradually dribble in the oil. The flavour of the oil will obviously deepen the longer it sits before using. Strain into a medium size frying pan and heat.

Add the croûtons and toss them in the flavoured oil over a moderate heat for about 1 minute, until evenly browned on all sides. Drain if necessary, cool and serve as a garnish for soups or salads.

FRUITY SALADS

One of the most striking and flavoursome additions to the already wide range of salad ingredients is that of fruit, and here there is also no shortage of variety. Yet the use of fruit in salad dishes, with a few exceptions like the well known Waldorf salad, is generally left to the dessert course and the collection of fruits in sugar syrup which forms the ubiquitous 'fruit salad', or more composed fruit dishes.

As a first course, fruit either simply on its own or in combination with other ingredients, can make a very light and refreshing introduction to the meal. If combined with fish, meat, egg and grains, it becomes more substantial and is ideal where a robust first course or an even more substantial main meal is required. At the end of the meal, the role of fruit in salad changes again, to produce a sweet but light and easily digested conclusion. This can be in the form of a liquid salad, such as fruit either poached or served fresh, in a light syrup, wine or fruit juice, or a fruit soup using one or more fruits. It can be a platter of prepared fruits with an accompanying purée of fresh fruits or fruit ice, or just simply a bowl or basket of unadulterated fruit. The fruits can also be moulded in jelly or used in combination with cheese to give a tasty combination of savoury and sweet.

Whatever the choice or preparation of the fruit, its position on the menu is ultimately a matter of individual choice and taste coupled with the way in which the ingredients are combined and dressed. Throughout the previous pages where the inclusion of fruit in a recipe seemed appropriate, I have used it, just as I have used other salad ingredients. In this chapter, however, the concentration is on fruit as the main ingredient for salads, whether as first or main course dishes, side salads or desserts. It is a patchwork of recipes and ideas; where you choose to slot them in on your menu will be a very personal choice.

INDONESIAN
FRUIT & VEGETABLE SALAD

SERVES

—— 4 ——

FOR THE SALAD

1 small fresh pineapple
1 crisp dessert apple
2 tablespoons lemon juice
7.5 cm (3 inch) piece
   cucumber, cut into
   5 mm–1 cm (¼–½ inch)
   cubes
175 g (6 oz) carrot, peeled
   and cut into 3 mm ×
   4 cm (⅛ inch ×
   1½ inch) sticks
100 g (4 oz) bean sprouts,
   washed and dried
2 tablespoons finely
   chopped, fresh coriander
   or flat-leaved parsley

**FOR THE SPICY PEANUT
   DRESSING**

2 tablespoons crunchy
   peanut butter
Juice ½ lemon
1 teaspoon ground
   coriander
½ teaspoon tabasco sauce
1 tablespoon soy sauce
4 tablespoons olive or
   sunflower oil

Many fruits and vegetables combine well to make interesting and tasty salads. This particular dish, with its spicy peanut dressing, marries pineapple and apple most successfully with cucumber, carrots and bean sprouts. It makes an excellent accompanying salad for other spicy dishes such as Indonesian satays or kormas as well as an attractive and unusual addition to the cold salad table.

Begin by preparing the fruit. Cut the top and bottom off the pineapple; cut off the skin, also removing the 'eyes'. Cut in quarters lengthwise, slice out the core and cut the flesh into 5 mm–1 cm (¼–½ inch) pieces. Place in a large mixing bowl.

Quarter the apple, remove the core and pips and cut the flesh into 5 mm–1 cm (¼–½ inch) pieces. Place in the bowl with the 2 tablespoons of lemon juice to prevent it from discolouring.

Add cucumber, carrot and bean sprouts to the fruit. Sprinkle on the chopped coriander.

Combine all the ingredients for the dressing in a bowl and when well blended pour over the fruit and vegetables. Toss well to mix, cover and leave to marinate for 15–30 minutes before serving in a salad bowl. The acidity in the pineapple tends to thin the sauce if left standing for more than 2 hours.

COLESLAW
FRUIT SALAD

SERVES

—— 4 ——

This unusual and refreshing combination, dressed in a light citrus dressing, makes an excellent addition to a selection of side salads for a simple meal or as part of a collection on a buffet table.

———

Divide the cabbage in half and cut out the core. Shred very finely into a large mixing bowl. Wash and dry the grapes, and if seedless and not too large, leave whole; otherwise cut in half and remove the pips.

Toss the apple pieces in the lemon juice to prevent from discolouring. Cut the skin and pith from the orange using a sharp serrated knife, leaving only the orange segments. Release these from the membrane by cutting between this and the flesh. Add the fruit to the shredded cabbage.

Pour on the citrus dressing and toss gently to moisten and combine. Season with a little freshly ground black pepper or a dusting of sugar to taste. Pile into a serving bowl and serve chilled.

INGREDIENTS

225 g (8 oz) white, hard-headed cabbage
100 g (4 oz) white grapes
100 g (4 oz) black grapes
1 eating apple, peeled, cored and sliced thickly
Juice of ½ lemon
2 oranges
3–4 tablespoons citrus dressing (p. 96)
Freshly ground black pepper or sugar

FRUITED BULGAR SALAD

S E R V E S

—— 4 ——

INGREDIENTS

75 g (3 oz) cracked/bulgar
  wheat
½ large cucumber, peeled,
  de-seeded and cut into
  5 mm (¼ inch) dice
2 tablespoons flat-leaved
  parsley, finely chopped
4 spring onions, finely
  chopped
1 clove garlic, peeled and
  crushed
1 tablespoon chopped, fresh
  coriander
2 tablespoons chopped,
  fresh mint
Juice of 1 lemon
2 tablespoons olive oil
1 teaspoon caster sugar
2 large fresh peaches or
  nectarines or 12 dried
  apricots, soaked if
  necessary
Freshly ground black
  pepper
Lettuce hearts or small
  crisp leaves

In this slightly sweet version of the traditional Lebanese salad *Tabbouleh*, soaked cracked wheat, also known as bulgar, is mixed with diced cucumber, fresh peaches, nectarines or dried soaked apricots. The salad is then moistened with a light lemon citrus dressing before being served in cups of firm, well shaped lettuce leaves.

Soak the cracked wheat for 20–30 minutes in enough cold water to cover, until the grains are tender and edible. Turn into a sieve and press out all the water.

Combine the cucumber with the parsley, spring onions, garlic, coriander and mint in a large mixing bowl. Add the soaked wheat and mix well.

Combine the lemon juice, oil and sugar in a screw-top jar, shaking well to blend. Pour over the salad and once again toss lightly to combine.

Cut the peaches or nectarines in half, removing the stones, and cut the flesh into 1 cm (½ inch) pieces. Add to the salad and toss gently to mix with the rest of the ingredients. Season with freshly ground black pepper if required.

Arrange the lettuce hearts or other firm crisp leaves around a salad bowl or plate and pile mounds of the fruited bulgar salad on each. This makes an excellent main course salad for a light lunch with wholemeal bread or an interesting addition to any salad selection.

WALDORF SALAD

SERVES

—— 4 ——

Waldorf salad is one of the classic salad combinations popular throughout the year, but particularly useful in winter when the delicate salad leaves are not so readily available. Created in America at the Waldorf-Astoria Hotel in New York, this tart crunchy combination of apple and celery makes it an excellent balance to rich meats and fish and an ideal salad for a buffet table.

Cut half of one apple into slices. Combine the lemon juice and sugar and dip the apple slices in the mixture to prevent discoloration; reserve these for decoration. Cut the remaining apples into 1 cm (½ inch) dice; place in a bowl with the rest of the sweetened lemon juice, toss well and leave to stand for 15–30 minutes while preparing the rest of the ingredients.

Add the celery slices to the diced apple with the walnuts. Pour over the mayonnaise, tossing gently to combine.

Line a serving bowl with washed and dried lettuce leaves, pile the salad in the centre of the leaves and garnish with the remaining apple slices. Serve chilled.

INGREDIENTS

450 g (1 lb) tart red dessert
    apples, quartered and
    cored
2 tablespoons lemon juice
1 teaspoon caster sugar
½ head celery, cut into
    5 mm (¼ inch) slices
50 g (2 oz) shelled
    walnuts, roughly
    chopped
150 ml (5 fl oz)
    mayonnaise (p. 100)
1 lettuce heart

CHICORY & ORANGE SALAD

S E R V E S
—— 4 ——

3 heads chicory
3 oranges
*3 tablespoons orange citrus
  dressing (p. 96)*
*Freshly ground black
  pepper*

This unusual salad with the slightly bitter taste of chicory combined with the sharp sweetness of the oranges makes a wonderfully refreshing salad which goes particularly well with rich foods such as pork, game, duck and stuffed meats. Carrot cut into fine shreds or sticks also makes an excellent addition to this salad.

Remove any slightly discoloured or browning outer leaves from the chicory and trim the root ends. Wash, drain and dry thoroughly, then cut into thin diagonal slices.

Cut the skin and pith from the oranges using a sharp serrated knife, leaving only the orange segments. Release these from the membrane by cutting between this and the flesh. Remove the pips and if the sections are large cut in half.

Combine the chicory and orange in a serving bowl. Pour over the citrus dressing and toss gently to combine. Season lightly with the freshly ground black pepper and chill well before serving.

BEETROOT SALAD

S E R V E S

—— 4 ——

A delightful refreshing and crunchy salad of grated raw beetroot, finely chopped celery and sultanas dressed in a light vinaigrette.

——————

Combine all the salad ingreidents in a large bowl and toss to mix well. Pour over the vinaigrette to moisten and toss again. Transfer to a salad bowl, cover and chill until required. This salad will keep for 2–3 days in the refrigerator.

INGREDIENTS

225 g (8 oz) raw beetroot, peeled and grated
2–3 celery stalks, chopped
1 small onion, peeled and finely chopped
50 g (2 oz) sultanas
1 tablespoon chopped fresh basil or 1 teaspoon dried basil
1 tablespoon parsley
3–4 tablespoons vinaigrette (p. 95)

TROPICAL FRUIT SALAD IN GINGER SYRUP

SERVES
—— 4 - 6 ——

FOR THE GINGER SYRUP
100 g (4 oz) granulated sugar
300 ml (10 fl oz) water
Juice of ½ lemon or lime
2 tablespoons ginger syrup from ready-made ginger in syrup
2 pieces of preserved ginger in syrup

FOR THE FRUIT
1 small pineapple
1 ripe mango
½ small perfumed melon such as ogen or charentais
1 pawpaw
1 kiwi fruit
8–12 fresh dates

Every cook, no matter how knowledgeable or wide their repertoire, has a few dishes which remain as outstanding favourites. I am no exception, and when a fruit salad is required and cost is not a major consideration, I opt for a combination of the wonderful variety of tropical fruits now so readily available – fruits which include mangoes, pineapples, pawpaws, fragrant melons and passion fruits and the large luscious fresh 'frozen' dates from Israel. These I float in a light syrup, flavoured with lemon or lime and slivers of preserved ginger. If funds are limited, only one or two of these fruits need be used, along with the ginger to bring a traditional fruit salad alive. In either of its forms, it never fails to be a success.

———

Make the syrup first so that it is absolutely cold before preparing the fruit. If time is very limited use apple juice instead of the sugar and water mixture. Put the sugar and water in a saucepan and warm over a gentle heat, stirring occasionally until the sugar has dissolved. Bring to the boil and cook for 4 – 5 minutes to form a sticky liquid. Add the fruit juice, ginger syrup and preserved ginger cut in thin slices. Pour into a large bowl and leave until cold.

Prepare the fruit, adding each to the ginger syrup in turn. Cut the top and bottom off the pineapple; cut off the skin, also removing the 'eyes'. Cut in quarters lengthwise, slice out the core and cut the flesh into chunky pieces.

Peel the mango and cut the flesh into pieces, removing the flat stone. Cut the melon in sections, remove the skin and seeds and cut the flesh into cubes.

Peel the pawpaw using a sharp serrated knife, cut in half and scoop out the seeds. Cut the flesh into quarters and divide into even sized pieces. Peel the kiwi fruit, cut in half lengthwise and then into 5 mm (¼ inch) slices. Remove the stones from the dates and quarter.

Stir the fruit to mix evenly and chill thoroughly before transferring to a glass bowl for serving.

NECTARINE,
YOGHURT & HONEY SALAD

SERVES

— 4 —

This salad of fresh nectarines mixed with chopped celery in a honey and yoghurt dressing, is a highly refreshing summer fruit salad either to be enjoyed on its own or served as part of a salad buffet. It can be made with peaches rather than nectarines, or a combination of both fresh and dried fruits such as apricots, raisins and pears. For a more substantial dish the salad can be served with cottage cheese.

———

Cut the nectarines or peaches in half and remove the stones. Cut into crescent-shaped slices. Cut the dates into slivers and toss with the celery in a large bowl.

Combine the yoghurt, honey, lemon juice and rind in a mixing bowl and beat until well blended. Pour over the fruit, celery and dates. Place a bed of crisp lettuce leaves in a shallow salad bowl and arrange the fruit mixture on top. Sprinkle with a little cinnamon and serve chilled.

INGREDIENTS

4 large ripe nectarines or peaches
8 stoned fresh dates
2 celery stalks, cut into 5 mm (¼ inch) slices
3 tablespoons thick set natural yoghurt
1 tablespoon liquid honey
Grated rind and juice of ½ lemon
Lettuce leaves to serve
1 teaspoon powdered cinnamon

Berry Fruit Salad

S E R V E S

— 4 —

A delicious and colourful combination of the berry fruits of summer – strawberries, blueberries, raspberries, redcurrants and blackcurrants – mixed with the sweet succulent flesh of the ogen melon and served as individual portions in the half melon shells.

Begin by preparing the sugar syrup. Put the sugar and water in a heavy pan and place over a gentle heat. Dissolve the sugar without letting the water boil and stirring only occasionally. Once the sugar has dissolved, add the lemon rind, bring the liquid to the boil and boil rapidly for 1–2 minutes. Leave to cool.

Prepare the fruit salad once the syrup is cold, transferring it from the saucepan to a large glass or china bowl; remove the lemon.

Cut the melons in half through their widest part, remove the seeds and, using a melon scoop (baller), scoop out as much of the flesh as possible. Drop these balls into the syrup together with their juice. Scoop out the remaining pulp to leave the shells hollow for the fruit salad. Put the shells in the refrigerator to chill.

Pick over strawberries, hull and if large cut in half lengthwise; pick over raspberries, blueberries and blackberries; wash red and black currants, dry on absorbent kitchen paper and remove from the stalks by running the prongs of a fork down the stems.

Add these fruits to the melon balls in the sugar syrup. Chill and just before serving fill each melon half with fruit salad and a little syrup. Decorate the centre of each with a small sprig of fresh mint. Serve chilled.

INGREDIENTS

FOR THE SUGAR SYRUP
*50 g (2 oz) granulated
  sugar*
150 ml (5 fl oz) cold water
A sliver of lemon rind

FOR THE FRUIT SALAD
2 ogen melons
*175 g (6 oz) mixed berry
  fruit: strawberries,
  raspberries, blueberries,
  red or black currants,
  blackberries*
4 sprigs of fresh mint

MIXED FRUIT COMPOTE

S E R V E S

—— 4 - 6 ——

This is a very quick and tasty fruit salad made from a combination of canned and fresh fruit and served in natural fruit juice or syrup enlivened with a little plum wine (available from Japanese or Chinese supermarkets). This fruit salad can also be made with fresh fruit poached in a sugar syrup (p. 120).

Combine all the canned fruit and their syrup or natural fruit juice in a large glass serving bowl. Wash the grapes and blueberries, dry gently on absorbent kitchen paper and add to the fruit bowl. If using black grapes wash, dry and remove the pips before adding to the other fruit. Stir in the plum wine and decorate with lemon verbena leaves.

INGREDIENTS

1 × 227 g (8 oz) tin of pear halves

1 × 227 g (8 oz) tin of peach halves

1 × 227 g (8 oz) tin of pineapple chunks

1 × 425 g (15 oz) tin of morello cherries, stoned

1 × 310 g (11 oz) tin of lychees

50 g (2 oz) seedless green grapes

50 g (2 oz) blueberries or black grapes

150 ml (5 fl oz) plum wine or a little liqueur

A few sprigs of lemon verbena

COMPOTE OF PLUMS IN
RED WINE SAUCE

SERVES
— 4 —

*300 ml (10 fl oz) red wine
or half red wine and port*
750 g (1½ lb) red plums
*4 tablespoons redcurrant
jelly*
*Grated rind and juice of 1
orange*
*2.5 cm (1 inch) piece of
cinnamon stick*

A delicious fruit salad can be made from the bright red plums of autumn. Care needs to be taken when poaching some varieties of plum such as the Victoria. These softer types will almost cook in the hot liquid. It is also optional to remove the stones.

Pour the wine into a large saucepan, bring to the boil and boil until reduced by half.

Meanwhile prepare the plums: wash and cut in half round the 'long' circumference and twist each half in opposite directions to separate from the stone. The stone generally remains in one half. Carefully ease this out with the point of a knife without doing too much damage to the plum. Alternatively leave the plums whole and unstoned.

Add the redcurrant jelly, the orange rind and juice along with the cinnamon stick to the wine in the pan. Stir over a gentle heat to dissolve the jelly.

Put the plums, rounded side down in the pan and let the syrup boil gently up and over the fruit. Reduce the heat and poach until the fruit is tender. This will take about 10 minutes. Transfer to a bowl and serve either hot or cold.

ORANGES IN
CARAMEL SYRUP

S E R V E S

—— 4 ——

This delicious dish of sliced oranges served in a rich caramel syrup makes a light and refreshing conclusion to any meal. Traditionally served in most Italian restaurants, the sweetness of the caramel sauce is counteracted by the tangy sharpness of the fruit. It is very quick and easy to prepare but is improved by sitting for a few hours before serving.

———

Make the caramel by combining the sugar and cold water in a large saucepan. Dissolve, without stirring, over a gentle heat. The water should not boil before the sugar has melted otherwise crystals may form round the edge of the pan and give a very granular cloudy and unsatisfactory result. When the sugar has dissolved, quickly bring to the boil and cook steadily until a rich golden colour. Once the colour is reached, immediately pour on the warm water. It is important to protect your hand with a cloth while doing this as the water hitting the caramel causes a lot of spitting and can be dangerous. Swirl the pot over the heat to dissolve any stubborn caramel, then allow to cool before pouring into a glass serving bowl.

Remove the peel from one orange using a potato peeler, to produce thin strips of peel. Cut into very narrow shreds. Cook the shreds in boiling water for a few minutes to remove their bitter flavour and make them curl. Refresh under cold water to set their colour. Use these to garnish the finished salad.

Remove the skin and pith from all the oranges using a sharp serrated knife. Cut each orange into thin circular slices and secure each in its original shape using cocktail sticks. Place in the cold caramel sauce, cover and chill well before serving sprinkled with the shreds of orange rind. Alternatively these oranges can be served simply in slices.

INGREDIENTS

4 large oranges

FOR THE CARAMEL SYRUP
225 g (8 oz) granulated sugar
150 ml (5 fl oz) cold water
150 ml (5 fl oz) warm water

123

SUMMER FRUIT GRATIN

S E R V E S

— 4 —

INGREDIENTS

2 large peaches or
nectarines, sliced
12 strawberries, halved
16 raspberries
A handful of redcurrants
and blackcurrants or 16
blackberries or
blueberries
1 young leaf of angelica,
finely chopped
2 tablespoons crême de
pêche, crême de cassis,
kirsch or Grand Marnier
(optional)
300 g (10 fl oz) double
cream
100 g (4 oz) demerara
sugar

One of my favourite summer fruit salads combines berry fruits with peaches or nectarines, along with a young leaf of angelica, and a fruit liqueur such as crême de pêche. Both the leaves and the liqueur take the sharp edge off the fruit. The cream is whipped until it holds its shape and is thick but not solid, before being spread over the fruit, dusted with demerara sugar and caramelised under a hot grill. It is served chilled and is utterly delicious.

Divide the prepared fruit between four small gratin dishes. Sprinkle with chopped angelica and liqueur.

Beat the cream until it begins to hold its shape, then divide between the dishes, spreading evenly over the fruit. Sprinkle the sugar in an even layer on top of the cream. Put the dishes on a baking tray and place under a hot grill for 6–8 minutes until the sugar has melted and caramelised. Allow to cool, then chill until ready to serve.

FRUIT SALAD KEBABS WITH YOGHURT & HONEY SAUCE

S E R V E S
—— 4 ——

These sweet fruit kebabs can be made with any combination of firm-fleshed fruit that can be easily threaded on to skewers, such as apples, pineapples, pears, peaches, nectarines, bananas or grapes, indeed almost any fruit which either takes your fancy or is readily available. The kebabs are served just as they are, or lightly cooked under a hot grill or over a barbecue fire with a yoghurt and honey sauce. The type of yoghurt used for the sauce is a matter of personal taste, but I prefer the natural 'thick set' yoghurt made from sheep's milk. This I find more tangy and much less rich and creamy than yoghurts made from full fat cow's milk.

Combine the orange rind and juice and the brandy in a large bowl ready to marinate the fruit as it is prepared and prevent it from discolouring. Prepare all the fruit as indicated. The seeds can be removed from the grapes by pulling the fruit off the stalk and using a sterilised hair clip impaled in a cork (and reserved for the purpose) to ease out the seeds. Cut the top and bottom off the pineapple and slice off the skin and eyes. Cut the pineapple in quarters lengthwise and cut out the core. Divide the flesh into similar sized chunks to the rest of the fruit. Leave the fruit to soak in the orange juice and brandy or liqueur for about 15–30 minutes.

While the fruit is marinading prepare the sauce by whisking the yoghurt and honey together and pouring into a serving bowl.

Thread the fruit on to kebab skewers, allowing two skewers per person. Lay each on individual serving plates with a pool of yoghurt and honey sauce to one side. Garnish with the mint leaves.

If the fruit kebabs are to be grilled, brush each with a little melted butter and cook over or under a strong heat for 5–8 minutes, turning frequently until the fruit is hot and beginning to colour slightly. Serve immediately in the same way as the cold kebabs.

INGREDIENTS

FOR THE KEBABS
Finely grated rind and juice of 1 orange
2 tablespoons orange liqueur or brandy
1 peach or nectarine, stoned and chopped thickly
2 large bananas, peeled and chopped thickly
1 large eating apple, quartered, cored and halved again
16 black grapes, de-seeded
1 miniature pineapple

FOR THE YOGHURT AND HONEY SAUCE
200 ml (7 fl oz) natural yoghurt
3 tablespoons liquid honey
A few sprigs of fresh mint

SALAD MENUS

*S*UMMER BUFFET

Fillet of beef niçoise (p77)
Traditional Coronation chicken
salad (p81)
Smoked mussel & rice salad (p86)
West coast salad (p76)

SALAD ADDITIONS

Green rice salad (p44)
Potato mayonnaise (p61)
Waldorf salad (p115)
Cauliflower & bean salad (p55)
Beetroot salad (p117)
Mesclun salad (p40)

Tropical fruit salad in ginger syrup
(p118)

*W*INTER BUFFET

Beef tapenade (p78)
Smoked mussel & rice salad (p86)
Chicken & beef satay salad (p83)

SALAD ADDITIONS

Mustard & dill potato salad (p63)
Carrot & nut salad (p54)
Chinese salad (p58)
Elegant coleslaw (p52)
Winter salad (p53)

Oranges in caramel syrup (p123)

*V*EGETARIAN BUFFET

West coast salad (p76)
Oriental salad (p75)
Tomatoes stuffed with guacamole (p28)

SALAD ADDITIONS

Brown rice & bean salad (p45)
Polish potato salad (p62)
Curried coleslaw (p50)
A classic green salad (p38)

Compote of plums in red wine sauce (p122)

CELEBRATION BUFFET

Salt beef salad (p79)
Chicken & pineapple salad (p82)
Salad niçoise (p84)
Greek salad (p73)

SALAD ADDITIONS

Mesclun salad (p40)
Curried pasta salad (p42)
Nutty coleslaw (p51)
Mushroom, mung bean & red pepper salad (p56)
Potato mayonnaise (p61)
Cauliflower & bean salad (p55)

Berry fruit salad (p120)

LIGHT LUNCHES

Tomatoes stuffed with guacamole (p28)
Caesar Salad (p74)

Greek salad (p73)
Tropical fruit salad in ginger syrup
(p118)

Crudités (p31)
Herrings in soured cream (p85)

Caesar salad (p74)
Mixed fruit compote (p121)

Tomato salad with feta cheese & basil
(p26)
Oranges in caramel syrup (p123)

*E*VENING MEAL

Pears in tarragon dressing (p29)
Salad niçoise (p84)

Bean & salami salad (p80)
Mesclun salad (p40)
Fruit salad kebabs with yoghurt & honey
sauce (p125)

Tomato, melon & cucumber salad (p27)
West coast salad (p76)

Spinach and dandelion salad with bacon
and croûtons (p36)
Chicken & beef satay salad (p83)
Nectarine, yoghurt & honey salad (p119)

Herrings in soured cream (p85)
Summer fruit gratin (p124)

INDEX

Italic page numbers refer to colour photographs